SCOTL
ULTIMATE GUIDE

Discover Scotland Iconic Attractions, Hidden Gems, Local Cuisine, and Practical Tips for an Unforgettable Journey

By

David M. Taylor

Copyright © 2025 by David M. Taylor

All rights reserved. No part of this book may be copied, shared, or used in any form without the author's written permission, except for short quotes used in reviews or academic work.

TABLE OF CONTENT

TABLE OF CONTENT 2
INTRODUCTION 6
   Welcome to Scotland 6
   Why Scotland Should Be Your Next Destination
   7
   A Brief History of Scotland 9
   Scotland's Unique Geography and Culture 10
PLANNING YOUR TRIP 13
   Best Time to Visit Scotland 13
   Entry Requirements and Travel Documents ... 17
   Budgeting for Your Scottish Adventure 19
   Packing Essentials for Scotland's Weather 22
   Health and Safety Tips 24
GETTING AROUND SCOTLAND 27
   Public Transportation: Trains, Buses, and
   Ferries 27
   Renting a Car: Exploring Scotland by Road ... 32
   Scenic Drives for Stunning Views 36
   Cycling and Walking Routes 43
EXPLORE SCOTLAND'S REGIONS 51
   The Scottish Highlands: Rugged Beauty and
   Outdoor Adventures 51
   Edinburgh: The Historic and Cultural Heart 58
   Glasgow: Scotland's Modern and Creative Hub
   64
   The Scottish Islands: Shetland, Orkney, and the
   Hebrides 71
TOP ATTRACTIONS IN SCOTLAND 78

    Edinburgh Castle 78
    The Royal Mile and Holyrood Palace 80
    Loch Ness and Urquhart Castle 84
    Stirling Castle and the Wallace Monument 87
    The Isle of Skye's Breathtaking Landscapes .. 91

OUTDOOR ADVENTURES 100
    Hiking the West Highland Way 100
    Climbing Ben Nevis: The UK's Tallest Mountain
    102
    Exploring Scotland's National Parks 104
    Wildlife Watching: Puffins, Red Deer, and
    Dolphins 106
    Stargazing in Scotland's Dark Sky Parks 108

SCOTTISH CULTURE AND TRADITION 111
    Scottish Festivals and Events 111
    The Art of Whisky Tasting: Scotland's
    Distilleries 115
    The Legacy of Clans and Tartans 121

HIDDEN GEMS OF SCOTLAND 129
    Glen Coe: Scotland's Scenic Treasure 129
    Eilean Donan Castle: A Fairy-Tale Fortress . 133
    The Fairy Pools on the Isle of Skye 138
    The Kelpies and Falkirk Wheel 142
    QUAINTS VILLAGES: PLOCTON AND
    CULROSS 147

DAY TRIPS AND WEEKEND GETAWAYS 155
    Visiting St. Andrews: The Home of Golf 155
    Discovering Inverness and the Great Glen ... 159
    Scenic Train Rides: The Jacobite Steam Train
    162
    Highlights of the Journey 162

Exploring the Borders: Abbotsford House and Melrose Abbey 164
ACCOMMODATION OPTIONS 168
    Luxury Hotels and Boutique Stays 168
    Castles You Can Stay In 173
    Pet-Friendly Stays 179
    Budget-Friendly Hostels and Camping Spots 183
DINING AND CUISINE IN SCOTLAND 190
    Traditional Scottish Dishes You Must Try 190
    Top Restaurants in Edinburgh and Glasgow 195
    Seafood and Coastal Delicacies 202
    Vegetarian and Vegan Dining Options..........208
PRACTICAL INFORMATION AND TRAVEL TIPS 213
    Currency, Tipping, and Language 213
    Emergency Contacts and Healthcare 215
    Driving Tips for Scotland's Roads 216
    Sustainable Travel Practices in Scotland......218
INDEX 222
LOCATIONS & COORDINATES 230
    Top Attractions 230
    Hidden Gems 231
    Accommodations 233
MAP/QR CODE 238

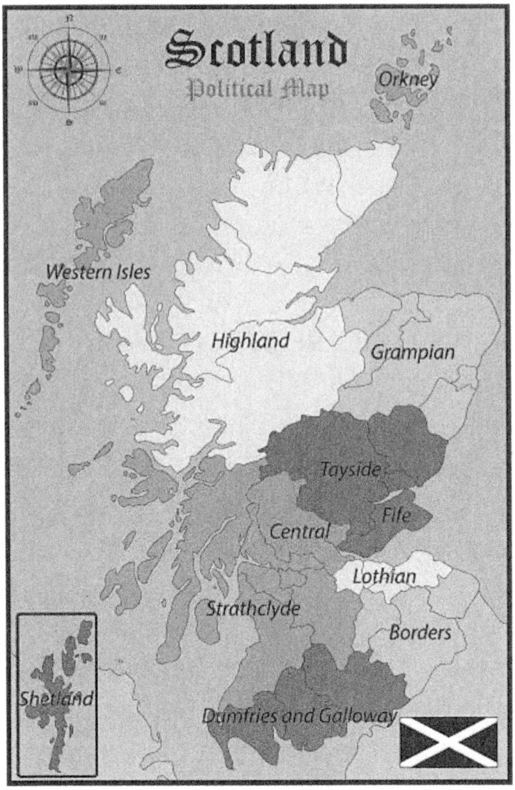
Scotland
Political Map
Orkney
Western Isles
Highland
Grampian
Tayside
Fife
Central
Lothian
Strathclyde
Borders
Shetland
Dumfries and Galloway

INTRODUCTION

Welcome to Scotland

Scotland is a place where history and natural beauty come together to create a truly magical destination. Known as the "Land of the Brave," it's a country filled with stunning landscapes, fascinating stories, and a lively culture that brings its cities and villages to life. Whether you're hiking through misty valleys, scaling towering mountains, or walking the lively streets of its cities, Scotland has something to offer every traveler.

The scenery is unforgettable, from the rugged peaks of the Highlands to the peaceful shores of countless lochs. Scotland is a land of contrasts, wild yet peaceful, ancient yet modern. Imagine hearing the sound of bagpipes in the distance, walking through ancient castle ruins, and ending the day with a warm meal in a traditional pub. A trip to Scotland isn't just a vacation; it's an experience that stays with you forever.

This guide will take you through everything that makes Scotland special, its rich history, its unique culture, its natural wonders, and helpful tips to make the most of your visit. Whether you're here for the first time or returning to uncover more hidden treasures, Scotland has new adventures waiting for you.

Why Scotland Should Be Your Next Destination

Scotland has everything you could want in a travel destination. Whether you love adventure, history, great food, or simply want to relax, this country has it all.

- **Incredible Scenery:** Scotland's landscapes are some of the most beautiful in the world. You'll find dramatic mountains in the Highlands, gentle rolling hills in the Lowlands, and even white sandy beaches in the Outer Hebrides. Don't miss places like Glen Coe, the Isle of Skye, and Cairngorms

National Park, they're absolutely breathtaking.

- **Rich History:** Scotland's history can be felt everywhere you go. Walk through medieval castles like Stirling or Urquhart, explore the cobbled streets of Edinburgh's Old Town, or visit ancient sites like the Callanish Standing Stones. Every corner of Scotland has a story to tell, bringing the past to life.

- **Unique Culture**: Scotland's culture is full of life and traditions. From Gaelic roots to clan history, you can see it in festivals like Hogmanay or the Edinburgh Festival Fringe. Traditional music, Highland Games, and whisky-making are just some of the experiences you can enjoy.

- **Outdoor Fun:** Scotland is perfect for outdoor enthusiasts. You can hike famous trails like the West Highland Way, climb Ben Nevis (the tallest mountain in the UK), or kayak along its rugged coastline. Scotland is also home to amazing wildlife, so keep an eye out for puffins, seals, and red deer.

- **Delicious Food and Drink:** Scotland's food scene is a mix of tradition and innovation.

Enjoy fresh seafood, hearty stews, and, of course, haggis. Pair your meals with a glass of Scotch whisky or a craft beer for a true taste of Scotland.

A Brief History of Scotland

Scotland's history is a long and fascinating tale of courage, determination, and progress. Thousands of years ago, Neolithic people settled here and built mysterious structures like Skara Brae and the Callanish Standing Stones, which you can still see today.

In the early centuries AD, Scotland was home to Celtic tribes and the Picts, fierce warriors who stood their ground against the Romans. The Romans eventually left, but they left behind signs of their time here, like the Antonine Wall.

During the medieval era, Scotland saw the rise of powerful clans and grand castles, symbols of its strength and independence. Figures like William Wallace and Robert the Bruce became national heroes during the Wars of Independence against England, shaping Scotland's identity as a proud and independent nation.

In the 18th century, Scotland became a center for intellectual and artistic growth during the Scottish Enlightenment. Thinkers like David Hume, Adam Smith, and James Watt made groundbreaking contributions to philosophy, economics, and science.

Even though Scotland joined the United Kingdom in 1707, it has kept its unique identity. It has its own legal system, education system, and strong cultural traditions that are still celebrated today. Scotland continues to honor its past while looking toward the future, making it a place where history and progress go hand in hand.

Scotland's Unique Geography and Culture

Scotland's landscapes are as varied as they are beautiful. It covers over 30,000 square miles and is divided into three main areas: the Highlands, the Lowlands, and the Islands.

- **The Highlands:** The Highlands are what most people picture when they think of Scotland. With towering mountains like Ben Nevis, tranquil lochs like Loch Ness, and dramatic valleys like Glen Coe, this area is perfect for anyone who loves wild, natural beauty.

- **The Lowlands**: The Lowlands offer rolling hills and fertile plains, dotted with charming villages and historic towns. This region is also home to Scotland's two largest cities, Edinburgh and Glasgow, where you'll find a mix of culture, history, and modern attractions.

- **The Islands**: Scotland has hundreds of islands, each with its own personality. From the mystical Isle of Skye to the Viking-influenced Orkney and Shetland islands, the islands are a must-visit for anyone looking to experience Scotland's diversity.

Scotland's weather is famously unpredictable, so it's best to pack for all seasons, no matter when you visit. Rain, wind, and sunshine can happen all in one day, which adds a little adventure to your trip!

The culture in Scotland is just as varied as its landscapes. You'll find a mix of ancient traditions and modern influences. The Gaelic language, tartan patterns, and bagpipe music are still alive today, alongside cutting-edge art, architecture, and a growing food scene. Festivals like the Edinburgh

Festival Fringe and Celtic Connections highlight Scotland's love of music, dance, and storytelling.

Scotland has also produced some of the world's greatest storytellers, from Robert Burns and Sir Walter Scott to modern authors like J.K. Rowling. Its rich literary tradition is celebrated through libraries, museums, and festivals, making it a dream destination for book lovers.

Everywhere you go in Scotland, you'll find stories, stunning views, and unforgettable experiences. It's a country that inspires curiosity, encourages exploration, and leaves a lasting impression on everyone who visits.

PLANNING YOUR TRIP

Best Time to Visit Scotland

Scotland is a destination you can visit at any time of the year, but the best season for your trip depends on what you want to experience. Here's a breakdown of each season to help you decide:

- **Spring (March to May):** Spring is a lovely time to explore Scotland, as the countryside comes alive with blooming flowers and lush green landscapes. Temperatures during this season usually range from 6–15°C (43–59°F), and the days start getting longer. Spring is perfect for outdoor activities like hiking, visiting castles, and spotting wildlife, especially the adorable baby lambs that appear in the fields.

- **Summer (June to August):** Summer is the most popular season for visiting Scotland. The weather is mild, with average temperatures between 15–20°C (59–68°F), and the long daylight hours mean you can enjoy more activities. In the northern parts of Scotland, you might even experience "White Nights," where the sun barely sets. This is the best time for festivals, such as the Edinburgh Festival Fringe, and outdoor adventures like kayaking, hiking, and exploring the islands. Keep in mind that summer is also the busiest time, so book your accommodation in advance, and always carry a rain jacket, as occasional rain showers are likely.

- **Autumn (September to November):** Autumn in Scotland is breathtaking, with the countryside transforming into shades of red, orange, and gold. The temperatures begin to drop, ranging from 8–15°C (46–59°F), and the tourist crowds thin out. This season is perfect for scenic road trips, visiting whisky distilleries, and stargazing in one of Scotland's Dark Sky Parks. It's also a wonderful time to take in the beauty of Scotland's national parks and enjoy crisp, cool air during your adventures.

- **Winter (December to February):** Winter in Scotland offers a magical experience, with snow-dusted mountains, warm and cozy pubs, and festive events. The temperatures usually range from -1–6°C (30–43°F), and you can enjoy activities like skiing in the Cairngorms, shopping at Christmas markets, and celebrating Hogmanay, Scotland's famous New Year festivities. Though the days are shorter, winter is a peaceful time to visit, especially for travelers who enjoy quieter surroundings and dramatic winter landscapes.

Pro Tip:

Scotland's weather can be very unpredictable, no matter the season. Pack layers of clothing, a waterproof jacket, and comfortable footwear to prepare for sudden changes in weather conditions.

Entry Requirements and Travel Documents

Traveling to Scotland is generally straightforward, but it's important to ensure you have the right documents before your trip to avoid any issues.

Visa Requirements:

- **UK and EU Citizens:** If you're a citizen of the UK or the EU, you don't need a visa to enter Scotland. A valid passport or national ID card is all you need.

- **Non-EU Visitors:** Travelers from countries like the United States, Canada, and Australia can visit Scotland without a visa for up to six months if they're traveling as tourists. However, you must have a valid passport. If you're planning to work or study, you'll need to check if a visa is required.

Always visit the UK government's official website to confirm the visa requirements based on your nationality.

•**Passport Validity:**

Make sure your passport is valid for the entire duration of your stay. Some countries may require your passport to be valid for at least six months beyond your travel dates, so it's always good to double-check these details before traveling.

•**Travel Insurance:**
Even though travel insurance isn't mandatory, it's highly recommended. It can protect you from unexpected expenses, such as medical emergencies, lost baggage, or trip cancellations.

•**Customs and Duty-Free:**
Scotland follows the UK's customs regulations. You're allowed to bring a limited amount of alcohol, tobacco, and other goods duty-free. If you're traveling from outside the UK, make sure to declare any items that exceed these limits to avoid fines or penalties.

Key Tips for a Smooth Entry:

1. **Keep Your Documents Accessible:** Always have your passport, boarding pass, and any required visas easily available for inspection at border control.

2. **Proof of Funds:** Although rarely requested, it's a good idea to have proof of

financial means, like a credit card or bank statement, to show you can support yourself during your stay.

3. Return or Onward Ticket: Some travelers may need to provide proof of a return ticket or onward travel to enter Scotland.

By ensuring your travel documents are in order and understanding the requirements for your trip, you'll be well-prepared to enjoy Scotland's incredible beauty and charm without any hassle!

Budgeting for Your Scottish Adventure

Scotland has something for everyone, no matter your budget. Whether you dream of staying in a grand historic castle or prefer a budget-friendly hostel, it's easy to plan your trip in a way that suits your finances. Thinking ahead about what you'll spend can help you enjoy your trip without worrying about money.

Average Costs You Should Know:

Accommodation:

- **Budget Options:** You can stay in hostels, budget hotels, or campsites for around £20–£40 per night.

- **Mid-Range Options:** Guesthouses, bed-and-breakfasts, and boutique hotels usually cost between £70–£150 per night.

- **Luxury Stays:** High-end hotels and historic castles start at £200 per night or more.

Food and Drink:

- **Affordable Meals:** Pub meals or takeaways typically cost £5–£10.

- **Mid-Range Dining:** Restaurants offer meals for about £15–£30 per person.

- **Fine Dining:** If you're looking for a fancy dining experience, expect to pay £50 or more per person.

- **Drinks:** A pint of beer usually costs £4–£6, and a glass of whisky is about £3–£5.

Transportation:

- **Public Transport**: Buses are affordable, with tickets costing £2–£4 per trip. Train fares vary but start around £10 for short trips.

- **Car Rental**: Renting a car typically costs £30–£50 per day, but this doesn't include fuel.

- **Fuel**: Petrol prices average £1.50–£1.80 per liter.

Attractions and Activities:

- Entrance fees to castles, museums, and landmarks are usually between £10–£20.

- Guided tours and special activities range from £30–£100, depending on the location and experience.

Budget-Friendly Tips:

- Use rail passes like the ScotRail Pass for unlimited train travel across Scotland.

- Explore free attractions like hiking trails, national parks, and some museums.

- Book accommodations and tours in advance for better prices.

- Visit local supermarkets or markets to grab affordable snacks or groceries.

Packing Essentials for Scotland's Weather

Scotland's weather is known for being unpredictable, so packing the right items will help you stay comfortable no matter what the day brings.

Clothing:

- **Layers Are Key:** Temperatures can shift throughout the day, so bring t-shirts, sweaters, and jackets that you can easily add or remove.

- **Waterproof Jacket:** Rain is common, so a good waterproof jacket is a must.

- **Comfortable Shoes:** Choose sturdy, waterproof walking boots for outdoor adventures and comfy trainers for city exploration.

- **Warm Accessories:** Even in summer, it's a good idea to pack a scarf, hat, and gloves, especially if you're visiting the Highlands or islands.

Other Essentials:

- **Travel Umbrella:** A compact umbrella is great for sudden rain showers but make sure it can handle wind.

- **Daypack**: Bring a small backpack for day trips to carry water, snacks, and other necessities.

- **Reusable Water Bottle:** Scotland has plenty of refill stations, so you can stay hydrated and avoid buying plastic bottles.

- **Adapter Plug:** Scotland uses Type G plugs (three rectangular pins) with a voltage of 230V.

- **Bug Spray**: During summer, midges (small biting insects) can be bothersome in rural areas, so bug spray is essential.

Pro Tip:

Don't worry if you forget something. Scotland's cities and towns have plenty of shops where you can pick up anything you missed.

Health and Safety Tips

Scotland is a safe country for travelers, but taking a few precautions will make your trip stress-free.

Health Tips:

- **Emergency Services:** If you have an emergency, dial 999 or 112. NHS Scotland provides free emergency healthcare for UK residents, but if you're from another country, make sure you have travel insurance to cover medical expenses.

- **Bring Your Medications**: Pack any prescription medications you need, along with a copy of the prescription. Pharmacies are widely available across Scotland.

- **Vaccinations**: Scotland doesn't require any specific vaccinations for entry, but it's always good to be up to date with routine vaccines like tetanus and flu.

Safety Tips:

- **Hiking and Outdoors**: Always check the weather forecast before heading out, especially in remote areas. Let someone know your plans and bring a map, compass, and plenty of water.

- **Driving Tips:** In Scotland, people drive on the left side of the road. Be extra careful on narrow, single-track roads, and always yield to oncoming traffic where required.

- **Wildlife**: When hiking or driving in rural areas, be mindful of animals like sheep or deer, which may wander onto roads.

- **Weather Awareness:** Scotland's weather can change quickly. Pack appropriate clothing and always have extra supplies when exploring remote areas.

Emergency Contacts:

- Police, Fire, or Ambulance: Dial 999 or 112.

- NHS 24 (for non-emergency health advice): Dial 111.

- Mountain Rescue: Available by calling 999 in case of an emergency during outdoor activities.

By planning your budget, packing for all kinds of weather, and taking a few safety precautions, you'll be ready for a smooth and enjoyable trip to Scotland!

GETTING AROUND SCOTLAND

Public Transportation: Trains, Buses, and Ferries

Scotland has a well-organized public transport system that makes traveling across cities, towns, and remote regions easy, affordable, and efficient. Here's a breakdown of trains, buses, and ferries to help you navigate Scotland smoothly.

Trains

Traveling by train in Scotland is not only convenient but also offers some of the most scenic routes in the world. Whether you're heading to major cities or exploring the Highlands, trains provide a relaxing and picturesque journey.

Popular Train Routes:

- **Edinburgh to Glasgow:** This quick route takes just 50 minutes to 1 hour, with ticket prices starting at £10 one way.

- **West Highland Line:** Known as one of the most beautiful train journeys in the world, this route from Glasgow to Fort William and Mallaig costs between £25–£50.

- **Inverness to Kyle of Lochalsh:** A stunning route that showcases the Highlands' beauty, with one-way tickets priced at £15–£25.

Ticket Costs and Options:

•**Advance Tickets:** Book online via ScotRail for discounts, with prices as low as £5–£10.

•**Rail Passes:**

- **Spirit of Scotland Travelpass:** Unlimited travel starting from £149 for 4 days.

- **ScotRail Travel Pass:** Offers unlimited travel on specific routes, ideal for tourists.

28

- **Children's Fares:** Kids under 5 travel free, and children aged 5–15 get discounted tickets.

Travel Tips:

•Travel during off-peak hours (outside morning and evening commutes) to save money.

•Consider upgrading to first class for more comfort, especially on scenic routes like the West Highland Line.

Buses

Buses are a cost-effective way to travel in Scotland, connecting major cities, smaller towns, and remote villages that trains don't reach.

City Buses:

- Cities like Edinburgh and Glasgow have extensive bus networks. A single ticket costs £1.80–£2.

- Day passes are available for around £4–£5, offering unlimited travel within the city.

Long-Distance Coaches:

•Operators such as **Citylink**, **Stagecoach**, and **Megabus** provide intercity services at affordable rates.

- **Edinburgh to Inverness:** Tickets start at £10–£20.

- **Glasgow to Aberdeen:** Fares range from £12–£25.

•These buses are equipped with Wi-Fi, charging points, and restrooms, making them comfortable for longer journeys.

Travel Tips:

•Book your tickets in advance to secure the lowest fares, especially with budget operators like Megabus.

•Carry exact change or use mobile apps like Lothian Buses for tickets in cities.

Ferries

Ferries are essential for reaching Scotland's many islands, such as the Hebrides, Orkney, and Shetland. The main operator is CalMac (Caledonian MacBrayne), with routes connecting mainland Scotland to the islands.

Popular Ferry Routes and Costs:

- **Oban to Mull:** £8–£20 per passenger and £30–£50 for vehicles (one way).

- **Ullapool to Stornoway (Outer Hebrides):** Tickets cost £15–£20 for passengers and £50+ for vehicles.

- **Aberdeen to Shetland (overnight ferry):** Prices start at £30–£45 for a seat, with cabins costing an additional £100 or more.

Travel Tips:

•Book tickets early, especially during peak summer months, as ferries can sell out.

•Check schedules carefully, as services may be less frequent during the off-season.

•Dress warmly and prepare for windy conditions on deck.

Renting a Car: Exploring Scotland by Road

If you want to explore Scotland's remote regions, scenic routes, and hidden gems at your own pace, renting a car is the best option. It gives you flexibility and access to places where public transport may not reach.

Car Rental Costs and Options

Rental Prices:

- **Economy Cars:** £30–£50 per day.

- **SUVs:** £50–£100 per day, ideal for rugged Highland terrain.

- Weekly rentals often come at discounted rates, starting at £200–£300 for an economy car.

Insurance:

- Basic insurance is usually included, but adding full coverage costs an additional £10–£20 per day.

Where to Rent:

- Major rental companies like Enterprise, Avis, and Hertz operate at airports and in major cities.

- Local companies like Arnold Clark often offer competitive rates and flexible policies.

Driving Costs

Fuel:

- Petrol costs about £1.50–£1.80 per liter, with a full tank typically costing £70–£100 for a standard car.

Tolls:

- Scotland has very few toll roads, with the main toll being the Forth Bridge near Edinburgh, which costs around £2.

Parking:

- **Cities**: Parking in cities like Edinburgh and Glasgow costs £2–£4 per hour. Park-and-ride services are more affordable at £4–£6 per day.

- **Rural Areas:** Parking is often free, but always use designated areas to avoid fines.

Tips for Driving in Scotland

1. Driving Rules:

- Drive on the left-hand side of the road.

- **Follow speed limits:** 30 mph in cities, 60 mph on rural roads, and 70 mph on motorways.

2. **Single-Track Roads:**

- Many rural roads are narrow with passing places. Be courteous and let oncoming vehicles pass.

3. **Weather Conditions:**

- Winter roads can be icy, especially in the Highlands. If visiting during this season, ensure your car has winter tires.

4. **Navigation:**

- Download offline maps or use a reliable GPS, as mobile signal may be weak in remote areas.

Choosing Public Transport vs. Renting a Car

When to Use Public Transport:

- If you're traveling between major cities or on a tight budget.

- For solo travelers or those not comfortable driving on the left side of the road.

When to Rent a Car:

- If you're visiting rural areas, scenic routes, or multiple destinations in one day.

- For families or groups who want flexibility and convenience.

By factoring in costs, convenience, and your travel plans, you can choose the best way to explore Scotland. Whether you take the scenic train routes or venture off the beaten path in a car, Scotland's beauty is sure to leave you amazed.

Scenic Drives for Stunning Views

Driving through Scotland is one of the best ways to soak in its incredible landscapes. With dramatic coastlines, rolling hills, majestic mountains, and tranquil lochs, every route is packed with breathtaking views. Here are some of the most scenic drives that will immerse you in Scotland's beauty:

North Coast 500 (NC500)

- **Route**: This famous 516-mile circular drive starts and ends in Inverness, taking you through the Highlands and along the rugged northern coast.

Highlights:

- **Bealach na Bà**: A winding mountain pass with jaw-dropping views of towering peaks.

- **Achmelvich and Durness:** Beautiful white sandy beaches, perfect for relaxing.

- **Dunrobin Castle**: A fairy-tale castle that's rich in history and architecture.

- **Ullapool and Dornoch:** Charming villages offering great food and local culture.

Tips:

- Allow 5–7 days to enjoy the route fully.

- Book your accommodations early, especially during summer, as it's a popular route.

The Road to the Isles

- **Route**: A 46-mile stretch from Fort William to Mallaig, with stunning views along the way.

Highlights:

- **Glenfinnan Viaduct**: Known as the "Harry Potter Bridge," a must-see for fans of the series.

- **Loch Eilt**: A serene and picturesque loch surrounded by greenery.

- **Silver Sands of Morar:** Beaches with pristine white sand and turquoise waters.

- **Mallaig Ferry Terminal**: Gateway to the Isle of Skye for an extended adventure.

Tips:

- Take your time to explore the small villages and hidden spots along the way.

- Spring and summer offer the best weather and scenery.

The Isle of Skye Loop

- **Route**: A circular drive around the Isle of Skye, starting at the Skye Bridge or ferry at Armadale.

Highlights:

- **Fairy Pools:** Crystal-clear waterfalls and rock pools surrounded by lush landscapes.

- **Old Man of Storr**: A striking rock formation perfect for hiking and photography.

- **Quiraing**: A dramatic landscape shaped by ancient landslides, offering fantastic views.

- **Neist Point Lighthouse**: Stunning coastal views and a great spot for sunset photos.

Tips:

- Spend at least 2–3 days exploring the island.

- Drive carefully on single-track roads, as they require patience and caution.

Cairngorms Scenic Route

- **Route**: A 90-mile journey through Cairngorms National Park, from Blairgowrie to Grantown-on-Spey.

Highlights:

- **Linn of Dee**: A gorge surrounded by woodland, ideal for picnics and short walks.

- **Balmoral Castle:** The summer retreat of the British royal family.

- **Aviemore**: A bustling hub for hiking, skiing, and wildlife watching.

- **Autumn Colors:** Vibrant shades of red, orange, and gold in the fall.

Tips:

- Autumn is the best time to visit for colorful scenery.

- Stop by local distilleries to sample Speyside whisky.

Southwest Coastal 300 (SWC300)

- **Route**: A 300-mile circular route in Dumfries and Galloway, in southern Scotland.

Highlights:

- **Mull of Galloway**: Scotland's southernmost point with stunning views from the lighthouse.

- **Sandyhills Bay**: A peaceful beach for a refreshing stop.

42

- **Galloway Forest Park**: A designated Dark Sky Park, perfect for stargazing.

Tips:

- This route is less crowded than the NC500, making it ideal for a quiet drive.
- Bring a picnic to enjoy at one of the scenic coastal spots.

Cycling and Walking Routes

Scotland is a dream destination for outdoor enthusiasts, offering cycling and walking routes that cater to all skill levels. Whether you're looking for a leisurely path or a challenging trail, Scotland's landscapes provide the perfect backdrop.

Cycling Routes

The Caledonia Way

- **Distance**: 235 miles from Oban to Inverness.

Highlights:

- Cycle along the shores of Loch Ness and soak in the legendary views.
-
- Pass through the Great Glen, a dramatic natural fault line.
-
- Explore Fort Augustus, a charming village with scenic canal locks.

Difficulty: Moderate to challenging.

Tips:

- Some sections have steep climbs, so be prepared.

- Plan for multi-day trips, as accommodations are available along the way.

The Hebridean Way

- **Distance**: 185 miles across 10 islands in the Outer Hebrides.

Highlights:

- Stunning beaches, rugged cliffs, and turquoise waters.

- Ancient landmarks like the Callanish Standing Stones on the Isle of Lewis.

- Unique island culture and local traditions.

Difficulty: Moderate, with some windy stretches.

Tips:

- Plan your route carefully to align with ferry schedules.

- Bring a repair kit, as bike shops are rare in the islands.

The Lochs and Glens Way

- **Distance**: 214 miles from Glasgow to Inverness.

Highlights:

- Ride through the Trossachs National Park and Loch Lomond.

- Enjoy incredible views of the Highlands as you approach Inverness.

Difficulty: Easy to moderate, ideal for families and beginners.

Walking Routes

West Highland Way

- **Distance**: 96 miles from Milngavie to Fort William.

Highlights:

- Traverse Rannoch Moor and the dramatic landscapes of Glen Coe.

- Finish at Ben Nevis, the tallest mountain in the UK.

- Cozy villages along the way offering warm hospitality.

Difficulty: Moderate to challenging.

Tips:

- Allow 6–8 days to complete the route.
- Wear sturdy boots and pack for unpredictable weather.

John Muir Way

- **Distance**: 134 miles from Helensburgh to Dunbar.

Highlights:

- Scenic coastal views and rolling hills.
- Historic sites like the Falkirk Wheel.

Difficulty: Easy to moderate.

Tips:

- Perfect for families or those wanting shorter hikes.

The Fairy Pools Walk

- **Distance**: 2.4 miles (round trip) on the Isle of Skye.

Highlights:

- Stunning waterfalls and crystal-clear pools.
- Suitable for all ages and fitness levels.

Tips:

- Arrive early in peak season to avoid crowds.

Pro Tips for Cycling and Walking:

1. Always carry essentials like water, snacks, a map, and weatherproof gear.

2. Be prepared for sudden weather changes, layers are key.

3. Stick to designated trails and respect nature by leaving no trace.

4. Let someone know your plans if you're heading into remote areas.

With its breathtaking scenery and variety of trails, Scotland offers unforgettable experiences for cyclists and walkers alike. No matter your level of experience, there's a route waiting to be explored!

EXPLORE SCOTLAND'S REGIONS

The Scottish Highlands: Rugged Beauty and Outdoor Adventures

The Scottish Highlands are one of the most remarkable and iconic areas of Scotland, known for their striking landscapes, fascinating history, and abundant wildlife. This region is perfect for travelers looking for outdoor adventures or a chance to connect with Scotland's wild beauty. Here's how to make the most of your visit to the Highlands.

Top Highlights in the Highlands

1. Loch Ness

- **Why Visit:** Famous worldwide for the mysterious Loch Ness Monster, this vast freshwater loch is surrounded by breathtaking scenery and intrigue.

Things to Do:

- Join a boat tour to explore the loch and maybe spot Nessie.

- Visit Urquhart Castle, which sits on the loch's edge, offering amazing views and insights into its history.

- Walk or bike along parts of the Great Glen Way, a long-distance trail with incredible views.

Best Time to Visit: May to September for warmer weather and longer daylight hours.

2. Glen Coe

- **Why Visit:** Known as the "Glen of Weeping," Glen Coe is a striking valley shaped by glaciers and volcanic activity, offering dramatic landscapes and historical significance.

Things to Do:

- Hike trails like The Lost Valley or Buachaille Etive Mor for incredible views.

- Learn about the Massacre of Glen Coe at the visitor center.

- Drive through the glen for awe-inspiring views and photography opportunities.

Best Time to Visit: Early mornings or late afternoons for fewer crowds and the best light for photos.

3. Ben Nevis

- **Why Visit:** As the tallest mountain in the UK, Ben Nevis is a must-visit for hikers and adventure seekers.

Things to Do:

- Hike the Mountain Track for a challenging but rewarding climb.

- Explore nearby Fort William, known as the "Outdoor Capital of the UK," for mountain biking and water sports.

Best Time to Visit: June to August when conditions are safer, but always check the weather before heading out.

4. Eilean Donan Castle

- **Why Visit:** This picturesque castle sits at the meeting point of three lochs and is one of Scotland's most photographed landmarks.

Things to Do:

- Tour the castle to discover its history and stunning architecture.

- Take photos at sunrise or sunset for the best lighting.

Best Time to Visit: Spring and summer when the surrounding area is lush and green.

5. North Coast 500 (NC500)

- **Why Visit:** This 516-mile circular road trip is one of the world's most scenic drives, showcasing the Highlands' diverse and dramatic landscapes.

Things to Do:

- Stop at remote beaches like Achmelvich Bay.

- Explore Dunrobin Castle and its beautiful gardens.

- Drive through the Bealach na Bà, a thrilling mountain pass with unforgettable views.

Best Time to Visit: May to September for clear skies and open accommodations.

Outdoor Adventures in the Highlands

1. Hiking and Trekking

- **The West Highland Way:** A 96-mile trail from Milngavie to Fort William with stunning views of lochs, glens, and mountains.

- **Cairngorms National Park:** Offers trails for all skill levels, from gentle woodland walks to challenging mountain climbs.

2. Water Sports

- **Kayaking and Canoeing:** Explore Loch Lomond or the River Spey for peaceful paddling adventures.

- **White-Water Rafting:** Thrill-seekers will enjoy the rapids of the River Findhorn.

3. Wildlife Watching

- Look for red deer, golden eagles, and otters in the Cairngorms or along coastal paths.

Pro Tip: Spend at least 4–7 days in the Highlands to fully experience its beauty and activities.

Edinburgh: The Historic and Cultural Heart

Edinburgh, Scotland's capital city, is a perfect blend of history, culture, and modern charm. From its medieval Old Town to its Georgian New Town, Edinburgh is full of iconic landmarks and unique experiences.

Must-See Attractions in Edinburgh

1. Edinburgh Castle

- **Why Visit:** Sitting atop Castle Rock, this iconic fortress offers incredible views of the city and a deep dive into Scotland's history.

Things to Do:

- View the Crown Jewels and the Stone of Destiny.

- Visit the National War Museum to learn about Scotland's military past.

- Watch the daily firing of the One O'Clock Gun.

Best Time to Visit: Arrive at 9:30 AM when it opens to beat the crowds.

2. The Royal Mile

- **Why Visit:** This historic street stretches from Edinburgh Castle to Holyrood Palace and is packed with shops, landmarks, and attractions.

Things to Do:

- Shop for Scottish souvenirs, including tartans and whisky.

- Visit St. Giles' Cathedral for its stunning Gothic architecture.

- Explore the Real Mary King's Close, an underground attraction that reveals what life was like in 17th-century Edinburgh.

Best Time to Visit: Late afternoon, when the street is lively but less crowded.

3. Arthur's Seat

- **Why Visit:** This extinct volcano in Holyrood Park offers some of the best views of Edinburgh and beyond.

Things to Do:

- Hike to the summit (about 1–2 hours round trip).

- Explore other areas of Holyrood Park, such as Salisbury Crags and St. Margaret's Loch.

Best Time to Visit: Sunrise or sunset for amazing views and fewer visitors.

4. National Museum of Scotland

- **Why Visit:** A family-friendly museum with fascinating exhibits on Scotland's history, culture, and innovations.

Things to Do:

- See the Lewis Chessmen, an important archaeological treasure.

- Learn about Dolly the Sheep, the first cloned mammal.

Best Time to Visit: Mornings or late afternoons to avoid crowds.

5. Princes Street Gardens

- **Why Visit:** A peaceful green space in the heart of Edinburgh, perfect for a break from sightseeing.

Things to Do:

- Admire the Ross Fountain and the famous floral clock.

- Enjoy views of Edinburgh Castle from the gardens.

Best Time to Visit: Spring and summer when the flowers are in full bloom.

Cultural Experiences in Edinburgh

1. Edinburgh Festival Fringe

- Held every August, this is the world's largest arts festival, featuring theatre, music, and comedy performances.

2. Ceilidh Dancing and Music

- Enjoy traditional Scottish dancing and live music at venues like The Ghillie Dhu or Sandy Bell's.

3. Whisky Tasting

- Visit The Scotch Whisky Experience or sample fine whiskies at local bars.

4. Literary Hotspots

- Edinburgh is a UNESCO City of Literature. Visit the Writers' Museum or The Elephant House, where J.K. Rowling wrote parts of Harry Potter.

Tips for Exploring Edinburgh

1. **Getting Around:** Edinburgh is best explored on foot, but buses and trams are available for longer distances.

2. **When to Visit:** August is great for festivals, while December offers Christmas markets and Hogmanay celebrations.

3. **Accommodation:** Stay in the Old Town or New Town for easy access to attractions.

With its wild Highlands and historic capital, Scotland offers two unforgettable experiences that will leave you in awe. Take your time in each region to truly appreciate their beauty and charm.

Glasgow: Scotland's Modern and Creative Hub

Glasgow is a city that embraces its industrial roots while thriving as a vibrant hub for art, music, and culture. As Scotland's largest city, it's filled with energy, creativity, and a welcoming atmosphere. Whether you love museums, live music, architecture, or shopping, Glasgow offers a perfect mix of modern attractions and historical charm. Known for its warm and friendly people, it's a city that feels alive day and night and has something for everyone.

Top Highlights in Glasgow

1. Kelvingrove Art Gallery and Museum

- **Why Visit:** This world-class museum is one of Scotland's most famous, with over 8,000 exhibits covering art, natural history, and Scottish heritage.

Things to Do:

- Admire Salvador Dalí's Christ of St John of the Cross, a standout masterpiece.

- Explore exhibits on Scotland's wildlife, archaeology, and cultural history.

- Take a relaxing walk through Kelvingrove Park, which surrounds the museum.

Best Time to Visit: Visit during weekday mornings for fewer crowds.

2. Glasgow Cathedral and the Necropolis

- **Why Visit**: Glasgow Cathedral is an awe-inspiring medieval structure, and the nearby Necropolis offers stunning views of the city and fascinating Victorian tombstones.

Things to Do:

- Wander through the cathedral to admire its Gothic design and learn about its religious significance.

- Explore the Necropolis, a sprawling cemetery filled with beautifully designed monuments.

Best Time to Visit: Late afternoon or sunset for a peaceful atmosphere and striking light for photos.

3. Riverside Museum and The Tall Ship

- **Why Visit:** This modern museum showcases Scotland's transport history and is paired with the historic tall ship Glenlee, docked outside.

Things to Do:

- See vintage cars, bicycles, and even old trams inside the museum.

- Step aboard the Glenlee to learn about life on a 19th-century sailing ship.

Best Time to Visit: Arrive mid-morning to explore both attractions without the crowds.

67

4. The West End

- **Why Visit:** Known for its bohemian vibe, this trendy area is filled with cobblestone streets, boutique shops, cozy cafes, and cultural landmarks.

Things to Do:

- Wander down Ashton Lane, a picturesque alley lined with pubs and restaurants.

- Visit the Botanic Gardens, which feature stunning Victorian glasshouses and peaceful walking paths.

- Enjoy a live performance at Oran Mor, a converted church turned cultural venue.

Best Time to Visit: Early evening for a lively dining and entertainment scene.

5. The Glasgow School of Art and Mackintosh Architecture

- **Why Visit:** Charles Rennie Mackintosh's Art Nouveau influence is everywhere in Glasgow, with the School of Art being one of his most celebrated creations.

Things to Do:

- Take a guided tour of Mackintosh's architectural works throughout the city.

- Visit the Mackintosh House, a restored home showcasing his unique designs.

Best Time to Visit: Book guided tours in advance, especially during peak tourist seasons.

Creative and Cultural Highlights in Glasgow

1. Live Music Scene:

- Glasgow is a UNESCO City of Music and offers live performances almost every night. Check out King Tut's Wah Wah Hut for intimate gigs or the Barrowland Ballroom for larger acts.

2. Street Art:

- The city's vibrant Mural Trail showcases incredible artwork on walls and buildings. Don't miss the famous Billy Connolly murals or the striking "Glasgow Tiger" near Ingram Street.

3. Shopping:

- Head to Buchanan Street for luxury and high-street shopping, or visit The Barras Market for antiques, vintage treasures, and unique finds.

4. Food and Drink:

- Try classic Scottish dishes like Scotch pies or Cullen skink at traditional pubs. Whisky lovers should visit The Pot Still, which offers an extensive selection of Scotch whiskies.

Tips for Exploring Glasgow

- Plan for 2–3 days to fully experience the city's attractions and vibrant atmosphere.

- Use Glasgow's subway system (nicknamed the "Clockwork Orange") for quick and easy travel around the city.

- Stay in the West End or Merchant City for convenient access to sights and great dining options.

The Scottish Islands: Shetland, Orkney, and the Hebrides

Scotland's islands are a world apart, each offering unique landscapes, ancient history, and rich cultural traditions. Whether you're exploring the remote Shetland Islands, the Neolithic treasures of Orkney, or the stunning beaches of the Hebrides, these islands provide an unforgettable escape.

Shetland Islands

The Shetland Islands, located far north of mainland Scotland, are a rugged and remote archipelago with a fascinating Viking history and incredible wildlife.

Highlights:

>1. **Jarlshof Prehistoric and Norse Settlement:** A site with over 4,000 years of history, featuring remains from the Stone Age through the Viking era.
>
>2. **Sumburgh Head**: Perfect for spotting puffins, seals, and whales during the summer months.

3. **St Ninian's Isle**: A picturesque sandy tombolo connecting the island to the mainland, ideal for walks.

Things to Do:

- Celebrate Shetland's Viking heritage at the Up Helly Aa fire festival in January.

- Take a wildlife cruise to see seabirds, seals, and orcas in their natural habitat.

Best Time to Visit: May to August for mild weather and abundant wildlife.

Orkney Islands

The Orkney Islands are a treasure trove of Neolithic wonders and breathtaking coastal scenery.

Highlights:

1. **Skara Brae**: A 5,000-year-old village that offers a glimpse into prehistoric life.

2. **Ring of Brodgar**: A massive stone circle that rivals Stonehenge in mystery and significance.

3. **St Magnus Cathedral:** A stunning medieval cathedral located in the heart of Kirkwall.

Things to Do:

- Tour Maeshowe, a chambered cairn perfectly aligned with the winter solstice.

- Learn about Orkney's wartime history at Scapa Flow, where naval wrecks lie beneath the waters.

Best Time to Visit: June to August for long daylight hours and warmer weather.

The Hebrides (Outer and Inner)

The Hebrides consist of over 100 islands, each offering jaw-dropping beauty, Gaelic culture, and unique attractions.

Outer Hebrides Highlights:

1. **Luskentyre Beach (Isle of Harris):** Famous for its turquoise waters and pristine white sand.

2. **Callanish Standing Stones (Isle of Lewis):** An ancient and mysterious stone circle.

3. **Barra Airport**: The world's only airport where planes land on a beach.

Inner Hebrides Highlights:

1. **Isle of Skye**: Known for the Fairy Pools, Quiraing, and Old Man of Storr.

2. **Isle of Mull:** Visit the colorful town of Tobermory and the historic Duart Castle.

3. **Isle of Iona:** Famous for its peaceful monastery and ties to early Christianity.

Things to Do Across the Hebrides:

- Explore hiking trails like the Skye Trail or the Hebridean Way.

- Take part in traditional Gaelic music festivals.

- Feast on local seafood like scallops and langoustines.

Best Time to Visit: May to September for pleasant weather and vibrant landscapes.

Tips for Exploring the Islands:

1. Use CalMac Ferries to navigate between the islands and mainland.

2. Pack layers and waterproof clothing, as the weather can change rapidly.

3. Book ferries and accommodations in advance during peak travel months.

From Glasgow's lively energy to the peaceful beauty of Scotland's islands, these regions offer something for every traveler. Spend at least 2–3 days in Glasgow and 5–7 days exploring the islands for a truly immersive Scottish adventure.

TOP ATTRACTIONS IN SCOTLAND

Edinburgh Castle

Why Visit

Edinburgh Castle is one of Scotland's most famous landmarks, sitting proudly on Castle Rock, a historic volcanic rock that overlooks the city. This ancient fortress has stood for centuries as a symbol of Scotland's history and heritage. With its incredible views and fascinating exhibits, it's a must-see destination for history enthusiasts and first-time visitors to Scotland.

What to Do

- **See the Crown Jewels:** Admire the Honours of Scotland, which include the crown, sword, and scepter used in royal ceremonies.

- **Explore the Great Hall:** Discover the medieval architecture and view the historic weapons and armor displayed there.

- **Visit the Stone of Destiny:** Learn about this ancient stone that was used in the coronation of Scottish kings.

- **Watch the One O'Clock Gun:** Witness the daily firing of the cannon at 1:00 PM, a tradition that dates back to 1861 (except Sundays).

- **Step into St. Margaret's Chapel:** Visit Edinburgh's oldest surviving building, built in the 12th century and beautifully preserved.

Best Time to Visit

- Arrive early in the morning when the gates open (around 9:30 AM) to avoid large crowds.

- Consider visiting at sunset for breathtaking views of the city, though it may be busier.

Ticket Information

- Adult tickets cost approximately £17.50, with discounts available for children, seniors, and families.

- It's best to book your tickets online in advance, especially during peak travel seasons, to skip long lines.

Pro Tip

The castle is located on a steep hill, so wear comfortable shoes for the climb. If needed, there is a shuttle bus available for visitors with mobility challenges.

The Royal Mile and Holyrood Palace

Why Visit

The Royal Mile is the historic heart of Edinburgh, stretching from Edinburgh Castle down to Holyrood Palace. With its cobblestone streets, historic buildings, and unique attractions, it's the perfect place to experience Scotland's history and culture. At the end of the Royal Mile, you'll find Holyrood Palace, the British monarch's official residence in Scotland, where you can explore the lavish royal apartments and beautiful gardens.

What to Do on the Royal Mile

1. Visit St. Giles' Cathedral: Admire the stunning stained-glass windows and Gothic-style architecture of this iconic church, also known as the "High Kirk of Edinburgh."

2. Take a Tour of The Real Mary King's Close: Go underground and learn about life in 17th-century Edinburgh in this preserved network of streets.

3. Discover the Museum of Edinburgh: Dive into the city's rich history, from ancient times to modern-day Edinburgh, through interactive exhibits.

4. See the Scottish Parliament Building: Appreciate the unique, modern architecture of this important government building near Holyrood Palace.

5. Shop and Eat: Explore stores selling traditional Scottish crafts, such as tartans, cashmere, and whisky, and enjoy delicious meals in cozy pubs along the way.

Visiting Holyrood Palace

- **Explore the State Apartments:** Walk through the grand rooms used for royal events, including the Throne Room and Great Gallery, where you'll find portraits of Scottish monarchs.

- **Visit the Ruins of Holyrood Abbey:** Marvel at the remains of this 12th-century abbey, surrounded by a peaceful atmosphere.

- **Stroll Through the Gardens:** Wander through the beautifully maintained gardens, offering a serene break from the busy city streets.

Best Time to Visit

- Visit the Royal Mile mid-morning when shops and attractions are open but crowds are lighter.

- Holyrood Palace is best visited early in the afternoon for a quieter and more relaxed experience.

Ticket Information

- Entry to Holyrood Palace costs about £18 for adults, with reduced prices for children, seniors, and families.

- You can also purchase combined tickets that include other Edinburgh attractions for better value.

Pro Tip

The Royal Mile is best explored on foot, so make sure to wear comfortable shoes. Plan to spend at least half a day to fully enjoy everything it has to offer.

These incredible attractions in Edinburgh offer a perfect mix of history, culture, and stunning sights. Whether you're exploring the towering Edinburgh Castle or walking along the historic Royal Mile to Holyrood Palace, these destinations are sure to leave lasting memories. Make sure to dedicate at least a full day to experiencing the magic of Edinburgh and its most famous landmarks.

Loch Ness and Urquhart Castle

Why Visit

Loch Ness is one of the most famous and mysterious places in Scotland, best known for the legend of the Loch Ness Monster, affectionately called "Nessie." This deep and dark freshwater loch is surrounded by beautiful landscapes, creating a serene and captivating destination. Sitting along its shores is Urquhart Castle, a historic fortress that adds drama to the scenery while offering incredible views of the loch.

What to Do

- **Take a Boat Tour:** Cruise across the calm, deep waters of Loch Ness. While taking in the stunning scenery, keep an eye out for Nessie, you never know what you might see!

- **Explore Urquhart Castle:** Wander through the ruins of this medieval stronghold, climb the towers, and enjoy sweeping views of the loch from its elevated position.

- **Visit the Loch Ness Centre and Exhibition:** Dive into the fascinating history of Loch Ness, learn about the search for Nessie, and discover the natural geology of the area.

- **Hiking and Picnics:** Stroll along the picturesque trails near the loch or relax with a by the water while soaking in the peaceful atmosphere.

Best Time to Visit

- Plan your visit between May and September to enjoy the best weather and long daylight hours, which are ideal for outdoor activities and boat tours.

- For a quieter experience, visit Urquhart Castle in the early morning or late afternoon when fewer people are around.

Ticket Information

- Entry to Urquhart Castle costs about £12 for adults, with discounted prices available for children and families.

- Boat tours on Loch Ness generally start at around £20 per person, though prices may vary based on the tour operator and trip length.

Pro Tip

Don't forget your camera, Loch Ness and Urquhart Castle are incredibly photogenic, especially at sunrise or sunset, when the light adds a magical touch to the scenery.

Stirling Castle and the Wallace Monument

Why Visit

Stirling Castle and the Wallace Monument are two of Scotland's most significant historic sites, located in the heart of the country. Stirling Castle was once the home of Scottish kings and queens, including Mary, Queen of Scots, while the Wallace Monument commemorates William Wallace, a national hero who played a key role in Scotland's Wars of Independence. Together, they offer an incredible journey into Scotland's medieval history and national pride.

What to Do at Stirling Castle

- **Explore the Royal Palace:** Walk through the beautifully restored rooms where Scotland's royalty once lived. The elegant interiors provide a glimpse into the lavish lifestyles of the past.

- **Visit the Great Hall**: Step inside this massive medieval banquet hall, one of the largest of its kind in Scotland, and imagine the grand feasts held here.

- **Step Inside the Chapel Royal:** Admire the intricate decoration of this historic chapel and learn about its significance in Scotland's religious history.

- **Interactive Exhibits:** Enjoy the Queen Anne Gardens and meet costumed guides who bring history to life with stories and demonstrations.

- **Take in the Views:** From the castle's battlements, enjoy sweeping views of the surrounding countryside, including the meandering River Forth.

What to Do at the Wallace Monument

- **Climb the Tower:** Ascend the 246 steps to the top of this iconic structure and be rewarded with panoramic views of Stirling, the Highlands, and the surrounding landscapes.

- **Learn About Wallace's Legacy**: Explore museum exhibits inside the tower that tell the story of William Wallace and Scotland's fight for independence.

- **See the Wallace Sword:** Marvel at this massive two-handed sword, believed to have been used by Wallace himself, which is on display inside the monument.

- **Walk the Woodland Trails:** Surrounding the monument are peaceful trails, perfect for a scenic walk and a chance to appreciate the natural beauty of the area.

Best Time to Visit

- Visit Stirling Castle in the morning to enjoy a quieter experience and explore at your own pace before heading to the Wallace Monument in the afternoon.

- The best time to visit is during spring and summer (April to September) when the weather is pleasant, and the outdoor spaces are at their best.

Ticket Information

- Tickets to Stirling Castle cost about £16 for adults, with discounts available for children, seniors, and families.

- Admission to the Wallace Monument costs around £10 for adults, with concessions for children and seniors.

Pro Tip

Combine a visit to Stirling Castle and the Wallace Monument into one day. They are located just a short drive apart, and the route offers stunning views of Scotland's rolling countryside.

Both Loch Ness with Urquhart Castle and Stirling with the Wallace Monument showcase Scotland's rich history and stunning natural beauty. Whether you're drawn to the legendary mystery of Nessie or the heroic tales of William Wallace, these destinations promise an unforgettable experience for any traveler.

The Isle of Skye's Breathtaking Landscapes

Why Visit

The Isle of Skye, often called the "Misty Isle," is one of Scotland's most stunning and magical destinations. It is known for its dramatic cliffs, rugged landscapes, sparkling lochs, and ancient legends. Skye offers a perfect retreat for nature lovers, photographers, and hikers. Its unique rock formations and charming villages make it a peaceful and inspiring place to explore.

What to See and Do on the Isle of Skye

1. The Quiraing

- **Why Visit:** The Quiraing, located on the Trotternish Ridge, is a must-see with its jagged peaks, rolling hills, and dramatic cliffs that stretch endlessly into the horizon.

Things to Do:

- Walk the Quiraing loop trail (about 4 miles) to enjoy incredible views and plenty of photo opportunities.

- Stop at key viewpoints to admire features like "The Needle" and "The Table."

Pro Tip: Visit early in the morning or late in the evening to avoid crowds and catch the best light for photos.

2. The Old Man of Storr

- **Why Visit:** This towering rock formation is one of the most recognizable natural landmarks in Scotland. Its striking appearance draws visitors from all over the world.

Things to Do:

- Hike the 2.5-mile trail to the base of the Old Man of Storr for incredible views of the surrounding landscape and the Sound of Raasay.

- Enjoy the peaceful surroundings and watch for wildlife, including deer and golden eagles.

Pro Tip: Sunrise is the best time to visit for a serene experience and breathtaking views.

3. The Fairy Pools

- **Why Visit:** These crystal-clear pools and waterfalls near Glenbrittle are magical, with their turquoise waters creating a fairy-tale setting.

Things to Do:

- Take the short, 1.5-mile trail to explore the pools.

- Dip your feet in the cool, refreshing water, or take a brave plunge for a quick swim.

Pro Tip: Wear sturdy shoes as the trail can get rocky and muddy, especially after rain.

4. Neist Point Lighthouse

- **Why Visit:** Located on the westernmost tip of Skye, this lighthouse offers dramatic views of rugged cliffs and the open sea. It's one of the best spots on the island for watching the sunset.

Things to Do:

- Walk the short trail to the lighthouse and enjoy the panoramic views of the coastline.

- Watch for dolphins, whales, and seabirds in the surrounding waters.

Pro Tip: Bring a warm, windproof jacket as it can be very breezy at Neist Point.

5. Dunvegan Castle and Gardens

- **Why Visit:** Dunvegan Castle, home to the MacLeod clan for over 800 years, combines rich history with stunning lochside views and beautiful gardens.

Things to Do:

- Tour the castle to learn about its history and view artifacts like the Fairy Flag, believed to bring good luck.

- Explore the gardens, including the Walled Garden and Water Garden, which are perfect for a relaxing walk.

- Take a boat trip from the castle to spot seals basking on the loch's shore.

Pro Tip: Visit in summer when the gardens are in full bloom for the most vibrant experience.

6. Portree

- **Why Visit:** Portree is the largest town on Skye and serves as a charming base for exploring the island. Its colorful harbor and lively atmosphere make it a highlight of any trip.

Things to Do:

- Stroll around the harbor and enjoy freshly caught seafood at local restaurants.

- Shop for unique crafts and souvenirs at small boutiques.

- Take a boat tour from Portree to see the coastline and spot marine wildlife.

Pro Tip: During the peak season, Portree can get quite busy, so make dinner reservations in advance to secure a spot at popular restaurants.

Best Time to Visit

- **Spring (April to June):** The landscapes bloom with vibrant colors, and crowds are smaller.

- **Summer (July to August):** Enjoy long daylight hours and great conditions for hiking and exploring.

- **Autumn (September to October):** The island's golden tones and quieter atmosphere make it especially beautiful.

- **Winter (November to March):** While it's colder, winter offers peaceful scenery and the chance to see snow-covered mountains.

Tips for Visiting the Isle of Skye

1. Getting There: You can drive across the Skye Bridge from the mainland or take a ferry from Mallaig.

2. Accommodations: Book your stay well in advance, especially during summer, as hotels and guesthouses fill up quickly.

3. Pack for All Weather: Skye's weather is unpredictable, so dress in layers and bring waterproof clothing and sturdy shoes.

4. Allow Plenty of Time: The island's narrow roads and frequent scenic stops mean you should plan for slower travel between destinations.

The Isle of Skye is a magical destination full of rugged landscapes, hidden gems, and charming towns. Whether you're hiking the Quiraing, marveling at the Fairy Pools, or exploring Portree, the island promises an unforgettable adventure. To truly experience its beauty and charm, plan to spend at least 2–3 days exploring this enchanting corner of Scotland.

OUTDOOR ADVENTURES

Hiking the West Highland Way

Why Visit

The West Highland Way is Scotland's most famous long-distance hiking trail. Stretching 96 miles from Milngavie to Fort William, this route showcases Scotland's diverse landscapes, from lush green fields and serene lochs to dramatic moors and towering mountains. It's an immersive way to experience the natural beauty of the Scottish Highlands.

Key Highlights

1. Loch Lomond Shores: Walk alongside Scotland's largest loch, with stunning views of its sparkling waters.

2. Rannoch Moor: A remote and hauntingly beautiful expanse of wilderness.

3. Glen Coe: Traverse one of Scotland's most famous valleys, with towering peaks and rich history.

4. Fort William: Finish your hike in the "Outdoor Capital of the UK" with views of Ben Nevis.

Trail Information

- **Difficulty**: Moderate to challenging. The trail includes flat sections, rolling hills, and steep ascents.

- **Duration**: Typically completed in 6–8 days.

- **Accommodation**: Options range from campsites and hostels to inns and bed-and-breakfasts along the route.

Tips for Hikers

- **Best Time to Hike**: Late spring to early autumn (May–September) for good weather and longer days.

- **Gear**: Wear sturdy hiking boots, pack layers for unpredictable weather, and carry a map and compass.

- **Pro Tip:** Book accommodations early, especially during the summer, as the route is popular with both locals and tourists.

Climbing Ben Nevis: The UK's Tallest Mountain

Why Visit

At 1,345 meters (4,413 feet), Ben Nevis is the highest peak in the UK. Climbing this iconic mountain is a challenging yet rewarding adventure, offering breathtaking views of the surrounding Highlands.

What to Expect

Routes:

> 1. **The Mountain Track (also called the Tourist Path):** The most popular route, suitable for most hikers, though it is still physically demanding.
>
> 2. **Carn Mor Dearg Arete:** A more challenging route for experienced climbers, with incredible ridge views.

Views: On clear days, you'll see across Loch Linnhe, the Highlands, and even as far as the Isle of Skye.

Tips for Climbers

- **Duration**: A round trip takes 7–9 hours, depending on fitness level and weather conditions.

- **Best Time to Visit:** June to September when the weather is more stable.

- **Safety**: Always check the weather before starting, as conditions can change rapidly. Bring plenty of water, snacks, and proper hiking gear.

Pro Tip: Start early in the morning to allow plenty of time to complete the hike before dark.

Exploring Scotland's National Parks

Scotland is home to two breathtaking national parks:

1. Loch Lomond and The Trossachs National Park

- **Why Visit:** Known for its picturesque lochs, dense forests, and rolling hills, this park is perfect for outdoor activities and relaxation.

Highlights:

- **Loch Lomond**: Enjoy kayaking, paddleboarding, or taking a boat cruise on Scotland's largest loch.

- **Ben A'an and The Cobbler:** Popular hikes with stunning summit views.

- **Falls of Dochart**: A beautiful waterfall near Killin, great for photography.

2. Cairngorms National Park

- **Why Visit:** The UK's largest national park, offering rugged mountains, ancient forests, and rare wildlife.

Highlights:

- **Cairn Gorm Mountain**: Hike or take the funicular railway for panoramic views.

- **Rothiemurchus Forest**: Ideal for walking, cycling, or wildlife watching.

- **Loch Morlich**: A sandy beach surrounded by mountains, perfect for picnics or water sports.

Pro Tip: Visit in spring or autumn for fewer crowds and mild weather.

Wildlife Watching: Puffins, Red Deer, and Dolphins

Why Visit

Scotland is a haven for wildlife enthusiasts, offering chances to see unique creatures in their natural habitats.

Key Wildlife

1. Puffins: Best seen from April to July on the Isle of May, Staffa, and the Shetland Islands. Watch them nest on cliffs and dive into the water for fish.

2. Red Deer: Scotland's largest land mammal, found in places like Glen Coe, Cairngorms National Park, and Isle of Jura. Autumn is the best time to witness the dramatic rutting season.

3. Dolphins: The Moray Firth near Inverness is one of the best places in Europe to see bottlenose dolphins. Boat tours offer up-close views.

Tips for Wildlife Watching

- Bring binoculars for better viewing.

- Wear warm clothing, especially for coastal tours.

- Respect wildlife by maintaining a safe distance.

Stargazing in Scotland's Dark Sky Parks

Why Visit
Scotland's low light pollution and remote locations make it one of the best places in Europe for stargazing. Designated Dark Sky Parks offer incredible views of the Milky Way, planets, and even the Northern Lights.

Top Stargazing Spots

1. **Galloway Forest Park**: The UK's first Dark Sky Park, perfect for seeing constellations and meteors. Visit the Scottish Dark Sky Observatory for telescopic tours.

2. **Cairngorms National Park**: Its secluded valleys and mountains provide excellent conditions for stargazing and occasional views of the Aurora Borealis.

3. **Isle of Skye**: Known for its dark skies, especially in areas like the Trotternish Peninsula.

Tips for Stargazing

- Visit during the new moon for the darkest skies.

- Dress warmly and bring a blanket or chair for comfort.

- Download a stargazing app to help identify constellations.

Scotland's outdoor adventures offer something for everyone, from challenging hikes and wildlife encounters to peaceful stargazing experiences. Plan your activities to make the most of the incredible natural beauty and rich biodiversity this country has to offer. Spend at least 3–5 days exploring these adventures for a truly unforgettable trip.

SCOTTISH CULTURE AND TRADITION

Scottish Festivals and Events

Why Experience Scottish Festivals?
Scotland is known for its lively festivals that celebrate history, culture, and traditions. From ancient customs to modern performances, these events showcase Scotland's unique spirit. Whether you're interested in music, art, or local traditions, Scottish festivals have something for everyone. These celebrations bring locals and visitors together, making them a great way to experience Scotland's warm hospitality.

Top Scottish Festivals and Events

1. Hogmanay (New Year's Eve)

- **Why Visit**: Hogmanay is Scotland's legendary New Year celebration, famous for its energy and scale. Edinburgh hosts one of the most iconic Hogmanay parties, with torchlight parades, live music, and stunning fireworks over Edinburgh Castle.

What to Do:

- Join Edinburgh's massive street party or watch the fireball-swinging ceremony in Stonehaven.

- Take part in "first footing," where the first visitor of the new year brings good luck to the household.

When: December 31st to January 1st.

2. The Royal Edinburgh Military Tattoo

- **Why Visit:** This world-renowned event takes place on the Esplanade of Edinburgh Castle. It features precision performances by military bands, Highland dancers, and musicians from around the globe.

What to Do:

- Watch the thrilling pipe bands and dance performances.

- Witness the grand finale with a lone piper playing atop the castle ramparts.

When: August (during the Edinburgh Festival season).

3. The Highland Games

- **Why Visit:** This traditional event is a celebration of Scottish heritage, featuring unique sports, music, and dancing. Events like caber tossing, tug-of-war, and Highland dancing are highlights.

What to Do:

- Cheer on athletes in traditional sports.

- Enjoy live bagpipe music and experience Highland culture.

When: Held from May to September in towns across Scotland (Braemar Gathering is the most famous).

4. Edinburgh Festival Fringe

- **Why Visit:** Known as the world's largest arts festival, the Fringe brings artists, performers, and comedians from around the world to Edinburgh. With thousands of shows in venues across the city, it's a creative spectacle.

What to Do:

- Watch experimental performances, stand-up comedy, and theater productions.
- Explore free street performances and interactive exhibits.

When: August.

5. Beltane Fire Festival

- **Why Visit:** This modern revival of an ancient Celtic festival marks the arrival of summer with fiery celebrations on Calton Hill in Edinburgh. Expect music, dancing, and costumed performances.

What to Do:

- Witness dramatic fire displays and storytelling through dance and drumming.

- Learn about ancient Celtic traditions and their connection to nature.

When: April 30th.

Pro Tip for Festivals

- Book tickets and accommodations early, as popular festivals like the Fringe and Hogmanay fill up quickly.

- Dress for unpredictable weather, especially for outdoor events.

The Art of Whisky Tasting: Scotland's Distilleries

Why Experience Whisky in Scotland?
Whisky, often called "Scotch," is deeply tied to Scotland's history and culture. With more than 130 distilleries spread across six whisky-producing regions, Scotland offers an incredible variety of

flavors and styles. Each distillery has its own unique character, and visiting them provides an inside look at the whisky-making process and the chance to taste some of the world's finest spirits.

Key Whisky Regions and Distilleries to Visit

1. Speyside

- **Why Visit:** Speyside is home to the most distilleries in Scotland, known for its sweet, smooth whiskies with fruity and nutty flavors.

Top Distilleries:

- **The Macallan:** Renowned for its luxurious single malts and modern visitor center.

- **Glenfiddich**: One of the world's most famous distilleries, offering excellent tours and tastings.

Pro Tip: Sample a whisky flight to compare different Speyside malts.

2. Islay

- **Why Visit:** Islay is known for its bold, peaty whiskies with smoky flavors that reflect the island's coastal environment.

Top Distilleries:

- **Lagavulin**: Famous for its rich, smoky single malts.

- **Laphroaig**: Offers detailed tours and a chance to become a "Friend of Laphroaig."

Pro Tip: Visit during the Islay Festival of Music and Malt in May for special tastings and events.

3. Highlands

- **Why Visit:** The Highlands produce a wide variety of whisky styles, from light and floral to rich and complex.

Top Distilleries:

- **Glenmorangie**: Known for its smooth single malts and innovative aging techniques.

- **Dalmore**: Specializes in premium whiskies with deep, complex flavors.

Pro Tip: Combine whisky tastings with visits to nearby castles or natural attractions.

4. Lowlands

- **Why Visit:** Lowland whiskies are known for their light, gentle character, making them ideal for beginners.

Top Distilleries:

- **Auchentoshan**: Famous for its triple-distilled whiskies.

- **Glenkinchie**: Located just outside Edinburgh, perfect for a day trip.

Pro Tip: Pair Lowland whiskies with desserts for a unique tasting experience.

5. Campbeltown

- **Why Visit**: Once the whisky capital of the world, Campbeltown has a small but proud whisky community producing distinctive malts.

Top Distilleries:

- **Springbank**: Known for its traditional methods and rich flavors.

- **Glen Scotia**: Offers whiskies with maritime influences.

6. Islands

- **Why Visit**: Each island produces whiskies with its own unique character, often smoky and influenced by the sea.

Top Distilleries:

- **Talisker (Isle of Skye):** Known for its bold, peppery flavors.

- **Highland Park (Orkney):** Balanced whiskies with hints of honey and smoke.

How to Enjoy Whisky Tasting

1. **Smell the Whisky**: Swirl the whisky and take a deep breath to pick up its aromas, like vanilla, fruit, or peat.

2. **Take a Small Sip:** Let the whisky rest on your tongue to explore its full range of flavors.

3. **Add Water:** A few drops of water can open up the whisky's hidden notes. Avoid ice, as it can dull the taste.

4. **Pay Attention to the Finish**: Notice how the flavors linger after you swallow.

Pro Tips for Whisky Tours

- Most distilleries require bookings in advance, so plan ahead.

- If visiting multiple distilleries, designate a driver or use local transport.

- Explore smaller, lesser-known distilleries for a more intimate experience.

Scottish festivals and whisky distilleries are at the heart of the country's culture. They offer a deep dive into the traditions, creativity, and craftsmanship that make Scotland so unique. By attending a festival or visiting a distillery, you'll leave with unforgettable memories and a greater appreciation for this fascinating country.

The Legacy of Clans and Tartans

Why Explore the Legacy of Clans and Tartans?

Scotland's clans and tartans are an important part of its history, culture, and identity. They represent loyalty, tradition, and the way of life of people who shaped the country's past. Clans were more than just family groups, they were powerful communities that influenced politics and land ownership. Tartans, with their colorful and unique patterns, symbolize the individuality of each clan and remain a proud part of Scotland's heritage today.

The Role of Clans in Scottish History

1. What Were Clans?

- Clans were extended families connected by shared ancestry, loyalty, and a sense of belonging.

- Each clan was led by a chief or chieftain, who was responsible for leading and protecting the group.

- While many members shared the same surname, clans also included non-relatives who pledged loyalty to the chief.

2. Historical Significance

- Clans played a key role in Scotland's history, especially in the Highlands, where they controlled land and managed local governance.

- Rivalries between clans often led to battles and alliances that shaped the country's past.

3. **The Jacobite Uprisings**

- Many Highland clans supported the Jacobite cause in the 17th and 18th centuries, fighting to restore the Stuart monarchy.

- After the defeat at the Battle of Culloden in 1746, strict laws were imposed to suppress Highland culture, including bans on wearing tartans and holding clan gatherings.

4. **Modern Relevance**

- Today, clan societies and gatherings celebrate Scottish heritage. These events allow people from around the world to reconnect with their Scottish roots.

The Importance of Tartans

1. **What Are Tartans?**

- Tartans are wool fabrics woven into plaid patterns that represent specific clans, families, or regions.

- Historically, tartans were used to identify clan members and show their allegiance.

2. How Tartans Are Made

- Tartans are created by weaving threads in horizontal and vertical patterns.
- The unique arrangement of colors and threads, called the "sett," defines the design of each tartan.

3. Tartan Revival

- After the Battle of Culloden, tartans were banned as part of efforts to weaken Highland culture.
- During the 19th century, tartans made a comeback, partly because of the romanticized portrayal of Highland life by authors like Sir Walter Scott.
- Today, tartans are proudly worn at Scottish celebrations such as weddings, Highland Games, and clan gatherings.

4. Famous Tartans

- **Royal Stewart Tartan:** The official tartan of the British royal family.

- **Black Watch Tartan**: A military tartan linked to the Highland regiment.

- **Clan-Specific Tartans:** Each clan, such as MacDonald, Campbell, and Fraser, has its own distinct tartan.

Experiencing the Legacy of Clans and Tartans Today

1. Clan Gatherings

- Clan gatherings happen all over Scotland and even internationally. They allow descendants to celebrate their heritage.

- Popular gatherings include those at the Clan Donald Centre on the Isle of Skye and events in Inverness.

- Activities often feature Highland Games, music, and storytelling about clan history.

2. The Scottish Tartan Register

- This official database keeps records of registered tartans. Visitors can find their family tartan and learn its history.

3. **Wearing Tartans**

   - Kilts made from tartans are an iconic part of Scottish culture, often worn during formal events like weddings and ceilidhs (traditional Scottish dances).
   - Accessories like scarves, shawls, and ties featuring tartans are also popular.

4. **Museums and Visitor Experiences**

   - **The National Museum of Scotland (Edinburgh):** Features exhibits on clans and tartans.
   - **The Tartan Weaving Mill (Edinburgh):** Lets visitors see how tartans are made and shop for authentic products.
   - **Culloden Battlefield:** Explains the history of the Jacobite Uprisings and their impact on clan culture.

Tips for Exploring Clan and Tartan Heritage

1. Research Your Ancestry

- If you have Scottish roots, look up your family surname to find your associated clan and tartan.

- Websites like Scotland's People can help trace your lineage.

2. Attend a Gathering

- Highland Games and clan gatherings are held across Scotland and are a great way to immerse yourself in traditional Scottish culture.

3. Buy Authentic Tartans

- Purchase tartan products from reputable shops or online stores. Always look for items made in Scotland to ensure authenticity.

4. Immerse Yourself in History

- Visit places like Eilean Donan Castle, a stronghold of Clan MacRae, or the Clansman Centre in Fort Augustus to learn about the lives of Scotland's clans.

The legacy of clans and tartans is an essential part of Scotland's identity. They tell stories of loyalty, strength, and tradition that have been passed down through generations. Exploring this heritage allows you to connect with Scotland's past while celebrating the traditions that continue today. Whether you're visiting a clan gathering, discovering your family tartan, or learning about the country's history, the experience is both fascinating and inspiring.

HIDDEN GEMS OF SCOTLAND

Glen Coe: Scotland's Scenic Treasure

Why Visit

Glen Coe, often called the "Glen of Weeping," is one of Scotland's most dramatic and picturesque valleys. Tucked away in the Highlands, it offers towering mountains, cascading waterfalls, and peaceful lochs that create a breathtaking and otherworldly scene. Beyond its natural beauty, Glen Coe is steeped in history, particularly the tragic events of the 1692 Massacre of Glen Coe, making it a place where nature and history collide in a powerful way.

What to See and Do in Glen Coe

1. **Hiking and Walking Trails**

    - Glen Coe is a dream destination for hikers, offering trails for both beginners and experienced adventurers.

    - **The Lost Valley (Coire Gabhail):** A moderate 3-mile round trip leading to a hidden valley used by the MacDonald clan to hide cattle. Its scenery is both dramatic and peaceful, making it a favorite among visitors.

    - **Buachaille Etive Mòr:** This pyramid-shaped mountain is one of the most photographed peaks in Scotland. It's a challenging climb but offers some of the most rewarding views in the Highlands.

    - **Pap of Glencoe:** This shorter but steep hike provides panoramic views of the valley and its surrounding peaks, perfect for adventurers seeking a shorter trek.

2. **Scenic Drives and Viewpoints**

    - **The A82 Road:** This iconic road through Glen Coe offers stunning views of cliffs, mountains, and rivers, making it one of the most scenic drives in Scotland.

- **The Three Sisters Viewpoint**: Stop here to take in the breathtaking view of the glen's three parallel ridges rising majestically from the valley floor.

- **Black Rock Cottage:** A small whitewashed building framed by the dramatic backdrop of the Highlands, often featured in postcards and films.

3. Historical Exploration

- **Glen Coe Visitor Centre**: This center provides insights into the glen's volcanic origins, its wildlife, and the story of the MacDonald massacre, a pivotal event in Scottish history.

- **MacDonald Memorial Site**: Pay respects to the MacDonald clan members who lost their lives in the massacre, marked by a solemn stone memorial.

4. Wildlife and Nature Watching

- Look out for red deer grazing in the lower valleys.

- Spot golden eagles soaring above the rugged peaks.

- Enjoy vibrant seasonal wildflowers that add color to the landscape, particularly in spring and summer.

Best Time to Visit

- **Spring (March–May):** Witness blooming flowers and enjoy quieter trails.

- **Summer (June–August):** Perfect for hiking and photography, though expect more visitors.

- **Autumn (September–November):** The golden hues of the glen make this season magical for scenic drives.

- **Winter (December–February):** The snow-dusted peaks offer serene and magical views, though hiking trails can be challenging.

Pro Tips for Glen Coe

- Bring waterproof clothing as rain is frequent in the area.

- Arrive early to avoid crowds, especially during peak summer months.

- Plan for at least a full day to enjoy the highlights, though multiple days are ideal for hiking enthusiasts.

Eilean Donan Castle: A Fairy-Tale Fortress

Why Visit
Eilean Donan Castle is one of Scotland's most iconic landmarks, sitting on a tidal island where three lochs meet, Loch Duich, Loch Long, and Loch Alsh. With its storybook-like appearance and stunning location, the castle is a favorite among travelers and

photographers. Beyond its beauty, the castle's history as a former stronghold of Clan MacKenzie and Clan MacRae makes it a fascinating place to explore.

What to See and Do at Eilean Donan Castle

1. Explore the Castle

- **Historic Interiors:** Step inside the castle to explore rooms restored with antique furniture, portraits, and weaponry that tell the story of the MacRae family and their role in Scotland's history.

- **The Keep:** Climb the spiral staircase to view exhibits detailing the castle's reconstruction in the 1900s after being abandoned for nearly 200 years.

- **Artifacts and Stories:** Discover relics such as the Fairy Flag and learn about the battles fought to defend the castle.

2. The Castle Grounds

- **Stone Bridge Walk:** Cross the picturesque bridge that connects the castle to the mainland, offering incredible views of the surrounding lochs and mountains.

- **Photography Hotspot:** The castle is a favorite among photographers, particularly during sunrise or sunset when the light enhances its dramatic setting.

3. Local History and Legends

- Learn about the castle's role in Scotland's turbulent history, including its destruction during the Jacobite risings in 1719.

- Hear legends about its ties to the Spanish Armada and its strategic importance during various conflicts.

4. Wildlife Spotting

- Watch for seals lounging on nearby rocks and seabirds flying above the lochs.

- If you're lucky, you may even spot dolphins or porpoises in the surrounding waters.

5. Dining and Shopping

- Enjoy a meal at the visitor center café, which serves traditional Scottish dishes and local snacks.

- Visit the gift shop to purchase tartan souvenirs, clan-related items, and crafts made by local artisans.

Best Time to Visit

- **Spring (March–May):** The surrounding hills are lush and green, making for beautiful photographs.

- **Summer (June–August):** Longer days and warmer weather make this a great time to explore, though it's the busiest season.

- **Autumn (September–November):** The castle is framed by warm fall colors, offering a quieter and more atmospheric visit.

- **Winter (December–February):** The castle and its surroundings take on a magical look with frost and snow, though hours may be limited.

Ticket Information

- Entry tickets cost around £10 for adults, with discounts available for children, students, and families.

- Book your tickets online during peak months to avoid waiting in queues.

Pro Tips for Eilean Donan Castle

- Visit early in the morning or late in the afternoon to enjoy a peaceful experience and the best lighting for photography.

- Check the tide schedule for the most dramatic views of the castle surrounded by water.

- Combine your visit with a trip to the nearby Isle of Skye, as the castle is conveniently located on the way.

Glen Coe and Eilean Donan Castle are perfect examples of Scotland's unmatched beauty and rich history. Glen Coe offers dramatic natural landscapes and a sense of serenity, while Eilean Donan Castle provides a glimpse into Scotland's storied past in a picture-perfect setting. Both destinations are must-visits, promising unforgettable memories for travelers. Spend a day or more at each to fully immerse yourself in their magic.

The Fairy Pools on the Isle of Skye

Why Visit

The Fairy Pools on the Isle of Skye are among Scotland's most stunning and magical natural attractions. Located in Glen Brittle, at the base of the Black Cuillin mountains, these pools are a series of crystal-clear waterfalls and deep turquoise basins that seem like something out of a dream. Their name reflects the otherworldly beauty they possess, drawing visitors who love nature, photography, and peaceful escapes into untouched landscapes.

What to See and Do at the Fairy Pools

1. Explore the Pools and Waterfalls

- Follow the Fairy Pools Trail, which is an easy-to-moderate walk spanning about 2.4 miles round trip. This path guides you past a collection of cascading waterfalls and serene pools.

- Each pool is unique, with shimmering turquoise waters and fascinating rock formations.

- Take a dip in the pools if you're up for it, though the icy waters are not for the fainthearted, the experience is unforgettable.

2. Photography Opportunities

- The Fairy Pools are a paradise for photographers, with vibrant blue-green waters contrasting against the rugged backdrop of the Black Cuillins.

- Visit during early morning or late afternoon to capture the best light and enjoy fewer visitors in your shots.

3. Wildlife Spotting

- Look out for wildlife like red deer grazing nearby, golden eagles soaring above, or otters playing in the streams. The natural surroundings add an extra layer of charm to your visit.

4. Picnic by the Pools

- Pack a picnic and relax near the pools. The sound of rushing waterfalls and the clean Highland air provide a perfect environment for a peaceful lunch.

How to Get to the Fairy Pools

- **Driving**: The pools are about a 30-minute drive from Portree, Skye's main town. Parking is available at the Glen Brittle car park for a fee of approximately £5.

- **Public Transport:** Public transport options are limited, so renting a car is the best choice for convenient access.

Best Time to Visit

- **Spring (March–May):** Fresh greenery and blooming wildflowers enhance the beauty of the area.

- **Summer (June–August):** With long daylight hours, this is an ideal season for exploring, though it tends to get crowded.

- **Autumn (September–November)**: The warm golden colors of fall create a magical atmosphere.

- **Winter (December–February):** Quieter trails and snow-dusted mountains make for a peaceful experience, but the paths may be slippery.

Pro Tips for Visiting the Fairy Pools

- Wear waterproof and sturdy footwear as the trail can be muddy, especially after rainfall.

- Bring layers and a waterproof jacket to stay comfortable in unpredictable weather.

- Arrive early to secure parking and enjoy a quieter experience.

- Allow at least 2–3 hours to explore fully and soak in the serene environment.

The Kelpies and Falkirk Wheel

The Kelpies

Why Visit

The Kelpies are two colossal horse-head sculptures, standing at 30 meters tall and located in Helix Park, Falkirk. They are the largest equine sculptures in the world, designed by artist Andy Scott as a tribute to Scotland's industrial heritage and the working horses that powered the canals and agriculture. These modern landmarks combine art, history, and engineering, making them a must-visit destination for anyone exploring Scotland.

What to See and Do at The Kelpies

1. Marvel at the Sculptures

- Walk around the towering Kelpies and appreciate their intricate steel design, which shimmers under sunlight or glows dramatically at night when illuminated.
- Their impressive height and reflective surfaces make them perfect for breathtaking photos.

2. Take a Guided Tour

- Join a guided tour to learn about the inspiration behind the sculptures, their construction process, and the cultural significance of working horses in Scotland.
- Step inside one of the sculptures to see its internal structure and understand the engineering behind it.

3. Relax in Helix Park

- Surrounding the Kelpies is Helix Park, an expansive green space with walking trails, a lagoon for kayaking, and picnic areas. It's an excellent spot for families and outdoor enthusiasts.

Best Time to Visit

- **Daytime**: Admire the details of the sculptures and explore the park at your leisure.

- **Evening**: Visit after sunset to see the Kelpies illuminated, offering a magical and atmospheric experience.

The Falkirk Wheel

Why Visit
The Falkirk Wheel is a unique and innovative boat lift that connects the Union Canal with the Forth & Clyde Canal, raising boats 35 meters. It's the only rotating boat lift of its kind in the world and a testament to Scotland's engineering expertise. The Falkirk Wheel isn't just functional, it's also a striking

piece of modern architecture set amid beautiful countryside.

What to See and Do at the Falkirk Wheel

1. Ride the Wheel

- Take a boat ride that demonstrates the Wheel in action. The trip provides panoramic views of the surrounding countryside and insight into how this impressive structure operates.

2. Explore the Visitor Centre

- The interactive exhibits and displays in the visitor center offer a fascinating look at Scotland's canal history and the innovative design of the Falkirk Wheel.

3. Walk or Cycle the Canals

- Stroll or bike along the nearby canal paths, which connect to the Wheel. These peaceful routes are perfect for enjoying nature and discovering historic sites like the Antonine Wall, a UNESCO World Heritage Site.

4. Family-Friendly Activities

- The surrounding area includes picnic spaces, a children's play area, and opportunities for water sports such as paddleboarding and kayaking.

Best Time to Visit

- **Spring and Summer (March–August):** Ideal for outdoor activities and enjoying the lush surroundings.

- **Autumn (September–November):** Vibrant fall foliage adds to the beauty of the area.

- **Winter (December–February):** A quieter time to visit, with reduced crowds, though boat rides may have limited availability.

Pro Tips for Visiting The Kelpies and Falkirk Wheel

- Combine both attractions into a single day trip, as they are only a 10-minute drive apart.

- Book boat trips at the Falkirk Wheel in advance, especially during peak seasons.

- Wear comfortable walking shoes for exploring the surrounding areas.

- Check opening hours for tours and visitor centers, as they may vary by season.

The Fairy Pools, Kelpies, and Falkirk Wheel each showcase Scotland's unique charm in different ways. While the Fairy Pools enchant with their natural beauty and tranquility, the Kelpies and Falkirk Wheel celebrate Scotland's cultural heritage and modern ingenuity. These hidden gems are sure to provide unforgettable experiences for travelers seeking both serenity and innovation.

QUAINTS VILLAGES: PLOCTON AND CULROSS

Plockton: The Jewel of the Highlands

Why Visit
Plockton is a charming village located on the shores of Loch Carron in the Scottish Highlands. Known as the "Jewel of the Highlands," it boasts a peaceful atmosphere, stunning views of the surrounding hills and lochs, and a unique charm enhanced by palm trees, thanks to the warm Gulf Stream. Plockton is the perfect destination for travelers who want to relax, explore nature, and experience authentic Highland culture.

What to See and Do in Plockton

1. Stroll Along the Waterfront
Take a relaxing walk along the picturesque harbor lined with quaint pastel-colored cottages. The still waters of Loch Carron beautifully reflect the scenery, making it ideal for capturing memorable photos.

2. Boat Trips and Wildlife Watching
Join a boat tour to explore the loch and nearby areas. Look out for seals lounging on the rocks, dolphins swimming playfully in the water, and various seabirds.

•Many boat tours are seasonal, so it's a good idea to check availability in advance.

3. Visit Local Art Galleries

- Discover small galleries showcasing the works of local artists inspired by the beauty of Plockton. It's the perfect place to pick up a one-of-a-kind souvenir or enjoy unique artwork.

4. Hiking and Exploring

- Take a scenic walk to Duncraig Castle, which offers stunning views of Plockton and Loch Carron.

- Drive to the nearby Applecross Peninsula and experience the breathtaking landscapes of the Bealach na Bà mountain pass.

5. Dining and Local Delicacies

- Savor fresh seafood at restaurants like the Plockton Inn or the Shores Restaurant. Don't miss the chance to try the village's famous langoustines and other locally sourced dishes.

Best Time to Visit Plockton

- **Spring (March–May):** Enjoy blooming flowers and mild weather.

- **Summer (June–August):** Ideal for outdoor activities, though it's the busiest time of year.

- **Autumn (September–November):** A quieter time, with golden hues enhancing the scenic beauty.

- **Winter (December–February):** Peaceful and serene, though some attractions may operate on reduced schedules.

Pro Tips for Visiting Plockton

- Parking can be limited, so arrive early during peak seasons.

- Bring a camera to capture the loch's stunning views.

- Spend at least a full day in Plockton, or stay overnight to fully appreciate its charm.

Culross: A Step Back in Time

Why Visit

Culross (pronounced "coo-riss") is one of Scotland's best-preserved medieval villages. Located in Fife, it feels like stepping into the 16th and 17th centuries with its cobblestone streets, whitewashed cottages, and orange-tiled roofs. Known for its role in the Outlander TV series, Culross is a must-visit for history buffs, photographers, and anyone who appreciates old-world charm.

What to See and Do in Culross

1. Culross Palace
Explore this historic building, which offers a glimpse into the life of wealthy merchants in the 17th century.

- Admire the beautifully restored interiors with period furniture and colorful painted ceilings.

- Wander through the palace gardens, filled with traditional herbs, flowers, and vegetables.

2. Wander the Cobblestone Streets

Take your time exploring the narrow streets of Culross. Admire the quaint houses with their orange roofs and colorful doors.

- Visit the Mercat Cross, the village's historic town square where markets were once held.

3. Culross Abbey

Discover the remains of this 13th-century abbey, perched on a hill overlooking the village.

- Learn about its ties to Saint Serf, an important figure in early Scottish Christianity.

- Enjoy breathtaking views of the village and the Firth of Forth from the abbey grounds.

4. Outlander Filming Locations

Fans of Outlander will recognize Culross as the fictional village of Cranesmuir. Explore sites like the Mercat Cross and Culross Palace, which were prominently featured in the series.

5. Tea Rooms and Souvenirs

Relax with traditional Scottish tea and homemade treats at one of Culross's cozy tea rooms.

- Browse local shops for unique crafts, handmade items, and souvenirs.

Best Time to Visit Culross

- **Spring and Summer (March–August):** The gardens are in full bloom, and the warmer weather makes it ideal for exploring.

- **Autumn (September–November):** The village takes on a magical charm with fall colors.

- **Winter (December–February):** A quieter season, though some attractions may have reduced hours.

Pro Tips for Visiting Culross

- Wear comfortable shoes for walking on the cobblestone streets.

- Plan to spend 2–3 hours exploring, though you may want more time to visit all the historic sites.

- Pair your visit with nearby attractions like the Forth Bridges or Dunfermline.

Why Visit Both Plockton and Culross?

Plockton and Culross showcase two distinct aspects of Scotland's charm. Plockton offers a serene Highland escape with stunning natural beauty, while Culross immerses you in the country's rich medieval history. By visiting these villages, you'll experience Scotland's incredible diversity, from tranquil landscapes to its vibrant past.

DAY TRIPS AND WEEKEND GETAWAYS

Scotland offers a variety of destinations that appeal to travelers of all interests. From historic landmarks to serene natural escapes, every corner of this beautiful country has something to discover. Whether you love history, nature, or charming towns, these day trips and weekend getaways are guaranteed to create lasting memories. Let's dive into four must-visit locations: St. Andrews, Inverness and the Great Glen, the Jacobite Steam Train, and the Scottish Borders.

Visiting St. Andrews: The Home of Golf

Why Visit St. Andrews?

St. Andrews, located in Fife, is known as the "Home of Golf" and is one of Scotland's most historic towns. Famous for its world-class golf courses, medieval ruins, and vibrant university life, it is a unique blend of rich heritage and coastal charm. St. Andrews isn't just for golfers, it's a destination where history and culture come alive.

Things to Do in St. Andrews

1. St. Andrews Links (The Old Course)

As the oldest and most prestigious golf course in the world, the Old Course is a bucket-list destination for golfers.

- **What to Do: Take** a guided tour of the course, even if you're not a golfer, to learn about its significance. Snap a photo on the famous Swilcan Bridge on the 18th hole.

- **Pro Tip**: To play, book your tee time months in advance or enter the daily ballot for a chance to secure a spot.

2. St. Andrews Cathedral

This medieval cathedral, now in ruins, was once Scotland's largest church.

- **What to Do:** Climb St. Rule's Tower for breathtaking views of the town and coastline. Wander through the graveyard and learn about the site's history in the visitor center.

3. St. Andrews Castle

Perched on a cliff overlooking the North Sea, this castle has a fascinating and turbulent history.

- **What to Do:** Explore the underground mine and countermine tunnels, visit the dungeons, and enjoy spectacular coastal views.

4. West Sands Beach

This iconic beach, featured in the movie Chariots of Fire, is a perfect spot for a walk or picnic.

- **Pro Tip:** Rent a bike or pack a kite to make the most of this vast, sandy expanse.

5. University of St. Andrews

Founded in 1413, this is one of the oldest universities in the world.

- **What to Do:** Explore the university's historic buildings, including St. Salvator's Chapel, and stroll through the beautiful Quadrangle.

Best Time to Visit

St. Andrews is lovely year-round, but spring and summer (April to September) are ideal for coastal walks and outdoor activities.

Getting There

- **From Edinburgh:** A 1.5-hour drive or 2-hour train and bus journey.

- **From Glasgow:** A 2-hour drive or 2.5-hour train and bus journey.

Discovering Inverness and the Great Glen

Why Visit Inverness and the Great Glen?

Inverness, the "Capital of the Highlands," is the gateway to some of Scotland's most dramatic landscapes. The Great Glen, a natural valley stretching from Inverness to Fort William, is home to lochs, forests, and historic landmarks, making it perfect for both adventure seekers and those looking to relax in nature.

Things to Do in Inverness

1. Inverness Castle

This iconic castle offers panoramic views of the city and the River Ness.

- **What to Do:** Visit the castle's viewing platform and enjoy a peaceful stroll around the grounds.

2. Inverness Museum and Art Gallery
Discover the history, culture, and geology of the Highlands.

- **Pro Tip:** Admission is free, making it a great budget-friendly stop.

3. River Ness and Islands Walk
This tranquil riverside walk takes you past small islands connected by charming footbridges.

- **What to Do:** Enjoy a quiet picnic or simply take in the serene views.

Exploring the Great Glen

1. Loch Ness and Urquhart Castle

Loch Ness is famous for its mythical monster, while Urquhart Castle provides a stunning historical backdrop.

- **What to Do**: Take a boat tour on Loch Ness or explore the castle ruins for incredible views.

2. Fort Augustus

Located at the southern end of Loch Ness, this village is known for its scenic locks on the Caledonian Canal.

- **What to Do:** Watch boats pass through the locks or enjoy a relaxing walk along the canal.

3. Outdoor Activities

- **Kayaking and Canoeing:** Paddle through the serene waters of Loch Oich or Loch Lochy.

- **Cycling**: Tackle the 79-mile Great Glen Way, which runs from Inverness to Fort William.

Best Time to Visit
Spring and summer (April to September) are perfect for outdoor activities, while autumn (October to November) offers spectacular fall foliage.

Getting There

- **From Edinburgh:** A 3.5-hour drive or train journey.

- **From Glasgow**: A 3-hour drive or train journey.

Scenic Train Rides: The Jacobite Steam Train

Why Take the Jacobite Steam Train?
The Jacobite Steam Train is considered one of the world's most scenic railway journeys. Running between Fort William and Mallaig, the route passes through breathtaking landscapes, including the famous Glenfinnan Viaduct, a key filming location for the Harry Potter series.

Highlights of the Journey

1. Glenfinnan Viaduct

Cross this iconic 21-arch viaduct while enjoying views of Loch Shiel and the surrounding Highlands.

- **Pro Tip:** Sit on the left side of the train when departing Fort William for the best views.

2. Loch Morar and Loch Nevis

These serene lochs showcase the untouched beauty of the Highlands.

3. Mallaig

The train's final stop is the picturesque fishing village of Mallaig.

- **What to Do:** Sample fresh seafood, visit the harbor, or catch a ferry to the Isle of Skye.

Ticket Information

- Tickets start at £49.50 for standard class and £72 for first class.

- Book well in advance, especially for summer trips.

Best Time to Ride

April to October is ideal, with summer offering clear views and autumn providing stunning fall colors.

Getting There

Fort William, the departure point, is accessible by car or train from Glasgow (3 hours).

Exploring the Borders: Abbotsford House and Melrose Abbey

Why Visit the Scottish Borders?
The Borders region is known for its rich history, stunning architecture, and peaceful countryside. Abbotsford House and Melrose Abbey are two must-see attractions that highlight Scotland's literary and religious heritage.

Abbotsford House: The Home of Sir Walter Scott

- **Why Visit:** This Gothic Revival masterpiece was the home of Sir Walter Scott, one of Scotland's greatest writers.

What to Do:

- Tour the house and see Scott's personal collection of books, weapons, and artifacts.

- Explore the beautifully landscaped gardens overlooking the River Tweed.

- Visit the visitor center to learn about Scott's life and works.

Pro Tip: Enjoy tea and snacks at the on-site café.

Melrose Abbey

- **Why Visit:** This medieval abbey is renowned for its intricate stonework and serene setting.

What to Do:

- Climb to the top of the abbey for panoramic views of the countryside.

- Look for the heart-shaped memorial said to contain Robert the Bruce's heart.

- Explore the museum to learn about the Cistercian monks who built the abbey.

Pro Tip: Early visits offer the best light for photography.

Best Time to Visit
Spring and summer are perfect for exploring gardens and abbey grounds, while autumn adds a romantic touch to the scenery.

Getting There

- **From Edinburgh**: Abbotsford House is a 1-hour drive, and Melrose Abbey is 1.5 hours away by car or train.

Final Tips for Day Trips and Getaways

- Plan your route and accommodations in advance, especially during peak seasons.

- Dress for Scotland's unpredictable weather by layering and bringing waterproof gear.

- Allow enough time at each destination to fully experience its charm.

Scotland's day trips and weekend escapes offer a diverse mix of history, culture, and natural beauty, ensuring unforgettable adventures for every traveler.

ACCOMMODATION OPTIONS

Scotland offers a wide variety of places to stay, catering to every kind of traveler. Whether you're seeking luxury, a unique castle experience, or more affordable options, there's something for everyone. Planning your trip early is crucial to secure the best rates and availability, especially during busy travel seasons. Here's a guide to help you find accommodations that match your budget and style, ensuring an enjoyable and memorable visit.

Luxury Hotels and Boutique Stays

Why Stay in a Luxury or Boutique Hotel?

Luxury and boutique hotels in Scotland provide top-notch services, elegant designs, and premium amenities. These accommodations often boast stunning locations, gourmet dining, and exclusive facilities like spas, private tours, or tailored experiences. Although they come at a higher price, they deliver an unforgettable stay.

Budget Overview

- **Luxury Hotels:** Prices generally range from £200 to £600+ per night, varying by location and time of year.

- **Boutique Hotels**: More affordable than larger luxury hotels, ranging from £150 to £300 per night.

Top Luxury Hotels in Scotland

1. The Balmoral Hotel (Edinburgh)

- **Cost**: Rates start around £350 per night.

- **Highlights**: Iconic location near Edinburgh Castle, Michelin-starred restaurant, and luxurious suites.

- **Money-Saving Tip:** Book during the off-season (November to March) for better rates.

2. Gleneagles Hotel (Perthshire)

- **Cost**: Rooms begin at £450 per night.

- **Highlights**: Famous golf courses, spa services, and breathtaking countryside views.

- **Money-Saving Tip:** Opt for a midweek stay, which is often cheaper than weekends.

3. Isle of Eriska Hotel (Argyll)

- **Cost**: Standard rooms start at £500 per night, with private suites costing £900+.

- **Highlights**: Located on a private island, offering fine dining and access to nature trails.

- **Money-Saving Tip**: Look for last-minute package deals, which may include meals or activities.

Top Boutique Hotels for Unique Experiences

1. The Witchery by the Castle (Edinburgh)

- **Cost**: Rates start at £350 per night.

- **Highlights**: Gothic-themed luxury rooms and proximity to Edinburgh Castle.

- **Budget Tip:** Book as far in advance as possible, as rooms are limited and highly sought after.

2. The Fife Arms (Braemar)

- **Cost**: Prices range from £250 to £400 per night.

- **Highlights**: Features contemporary art, a Highland setting, and a cozy yet luxurious vibe.

- **Money-Saving Tip:** Watch for meal-inclusive packages to maximize value.

3. Killiehuntly Farmhouse (Cairngorms National Park)

- **Cost**: Rooms start at £200 per night.

- **Highlights**: Combines Scandinavian minimalism with traditional Highland charm.

- **Budget Tip:** Choose one of their smaller cottages for lower rates without compromising comfort.

Castles You Can Stay In

Why Stay in a Castle?

Staying in a Scottish castle offers an enchanting experience steeped in history. These properties provide the perfect mix of modern luxury and timeless architecture, giving visitors a chance to step back in time while enjoying top-tier amenities.

Budget Overview

- **Castle Stays**: Prices typically range from £250 to £700+ per night, depending on the size, location, and exclusivity.

- **Exclusive Rentals**: Entire castle rentals start from £2,000 per night, ideal for large groups or special occasions.

Top Castles to Stay In

1. Inverlochy Castle Hotel (Fort William)

- **Cost**: Rooms start at £400 per night.

- **Highlights**: Elegant suites, gourmet dining, and breathtaking Highland surroundings.

- **Money-Saving Tip:** Check for packages that include meals or outdoor activities.

2. Dalhousie Castle (Near Edinburgh)

- **Cost**: Prices start at £300 per night.

- **Highlights**: Dungeon spa, historic rooms, and falconry experiences.

- **Budget Tip:** Midweek bookings are generally cheaper.

3. Barcaldine Castle (Argyll)

- **Cost**: Rooms begin at £250 per night.

- **Highlights**: Intimate accommodations with stunning views of Loch Creran.

- **Money-Saving Tip:** Visit during the off-season (November to February) for lower prices.

4. Borthwick Castle (Near Edinburgh)

- **Cost**: Exclusive rentals start at £3,000 per night.

- **Highlights**: Luxurious period interiors and private events in a historic setting.

- **Budget Tip:** Split the cost with a group to make the stay more affordable.

Tips for Budgeting a Castle Stay

1. Travel Off-Peak: Rates are lower in the winter months, and crowds are smaller.

2. Consider Meal Packages: Some castles offer breakfast or dinner-inclusive packages, reducing dining expenses.

3. Explore Day Options: Many castles offer day tours and afternoon tea for those who want to experience the grandeur without staying overnight.

Planning Your Accommodation Budget

Average Costs in Scotland

- **Hostels and Budget Hotels:** £20–£60 per night.

- **Mid-Range Hotels:** £80–£150 per night.

- **Luxury Hotels and Castle Stays:** £200–£600+ per night.

Smart Ways to Save on Accommodations

1. Book Early: Popular destinations like Edinburgh or the Isle of Skye fill up fast. Secure your spot months ahead.

2. Travel in the Off-Season: Late autumn and winter offer lower rates for hotels and castles.

3. Stay Longer: Some accommodations provide discounts for extended stays.

4. Use Discount Platforms: Sites like Booking.com or Airbnb often feature special offers and deals.

Other Considerations for Planning Your Stay

Location Matters

- Staying in city centers offers easy access to attractions but comes with higher costs.

- Rural areas and smaller villages provide quieter settings and more budget-friendly options.

Transportation

- Ensure your accommodation has parking if you're driving.

- Check for nearby public transport options if you don't plan to drive.

Amenities

- Look for places that include free breakfast, Wi-Fi, or other perks like guided tours or activity passes.

Pet-Friendly Stays

Why Choose Pet-Friendly Accommodation?

If you want to bring your furry friends along to explore Scotland's stunning landscapes, pet-friendly accommodations are the perfect option. From cozy countryside inns to luxury hotels, many places in Scotland are happy to welcome pets, ensuring you and your companion have a memorable trip.

What You'll Find in Pet-Friendly Stays

- **Costs**: Expect to pay an extra £10–£25 per night per pet for their stay.

- **Facilities**: Accommodations often include amenities like dog beds, food bowls, and outdoor spaces for exercise.

- **Locations**: Many pet-friendly places are close to beaches, parks, and walking trails, making it easier to plan outdoor activities.

Top Pet-Friendly Accommodations in Scotland

1. The Four Seasons Hotel (Loch Earn)

- **Cost**: Rooms start at £150 per night, with a £15 pet fee per night.

- **Why Stay Here:** Set by a beautiful loch, this hotel features scenic walking trails and even dog-friendly dining options.

- **Travel Tip**: Request a ground-floor room for convenient outdoor access.

2. The Fife Arms (Braemar)

- **Cost**: Rates start at £250 per night, with a £20 fee per pet.

- **Why Stay Here:** Located in the Cairngorms National Park, this boutique hotel is ideal for hiking enthusiasts traveling with pets.

- **Travel Tip:** Book well in advance since their pet-friendly rooms are limited.

3. The Inn on the Tay (Pitlochry)

- **Cost**: Rooms start at £120 per night, with a £10 fee per pet.

- **Why Stay Here**: Situated along the River Tay, this inn offers plenty of nearby trails and dog-friendly pubs.

- **Travel Tip:** Take advantage of their dog-friendly dining areas for a stress-free meal.

Pet-Friendly Cottages and Cabins

1. Unique Cottages Scotland

- **Cost**: Weekly rentals start at £350, depending on location and size.

- **Why Stay Here**: Many cottages feature enclosed gardens, ideal for pets, and are located near dog-friendly beaches or forests.

2. **Wigwam Holidays**

- **Cost**: Glamping pods start at £70 per night, with a £10 pet fee per stay.

- **Why Stay Here:** Perfect for those who want a unique, nature-filled stay with their pets.

Tips for Traveling with Pets in Scotland

1. Check Rules: Some accommodations have restrictions on pet size or may not allow pets to be left unattended.

2. Pack Essentials: Bring along your pet's bed, food, leash, and favorite toys for a smoother stay.

3. Choose Activities Nearby: Stay close to walking trails, beaches, or pet-friendly parks to keep your companion active and happy.

Budget-Friendly Hostels and Camping Spots

Why Choose Budget Accommodations?

Traveling on a budget doesn't mean missing out on Scotland's beauty and culture. Hostels and campsites offer affordable, comfortable options for travelers while encouraging a sense of community and connection to nature.

What to Expect

- **Hostels**: Dorm beds cost between £20–£40 per night, while private rooms range from £50–£80 per night.

- **Camping**: Tent pitches typically range from £10–£25 per night, depending on location and amenities.

- **Facilities**: Hostels often feature shared kitchens, free Wi-Fi, and communal lounges, while campsites include basic facilities like showers, toilets, and outdoor cooking areas.

Top Hostels in Scotland

1. Castle Rock Hostel (Edinburgh)

- **Cost**: Dorm beds from £25 per night, private rooms from £50 per night.

- **Why Stay Here**: Centrally located near Edinburgh Castle, it's a lively and social hostel.

- **Pro Tip:** Book early during festival season to secure your spot.

2. **Skye Basecamp (Isle of Skye)**

- **Cost**: Dorm beds from £28 per night.

- **Why Stay Here:** Close to famous Skye attractions like the Fairy Pools and the Quiraing, this hostel is perfect for outdoor lovers.

- **Pro Tip:** Use the shared kitchen to save on dining costs.

3. Oban Youth Hostel (Oban)

- **Cost**: Dorm beds start at £30 per night, private rooms at £60 per night.

- **Why Stay Here:** Located on the waterfront, this hostel offers spectacular sea views.

- **Pro Tip:** Don't miss their affordable breakfast options.

Best Camping Spots in Scotland

1. Loch Lomond and The Trossachs National Park

- **Cost**: Tent pitches start at £15 per night.

- **Why Stay Here:** Stunning views of lochs and hills with plenty of kayaking and hiking opportunities.

- **Pro Tip**: Choose a campsite near the water for sunrise views.

2. Glen Nevis Campsite (Near Ben Nevis)

- **Cost**: Tent pitches from £20 per night.

- **Why Stay Here:** Perfect for adventurers planning to climb Ben Nevis.

- **Pro Tip:** Arrive early to secure a pitch at this popular campsite.

3. Red Squirrel Campsite (Glen Coe)

- **Cost**: Rates start at £12 per person per night.
- **Why Stay Here:** Surrounded by dramatic Highland scenery and close to hiking trails.
- **Pro Tip:** Pack waterproof gear as the weather in Glen Coe is unpredictable.

Tips for Saving Money on Budget Accommodations

1. Book Early: Popular hostels and campsites fill up quickly, especially in summer.

2. Take Advantage of Passes: Look for discounts through organizations like Hostelling Scotland.

3. Cook Your Own Meals: Use hostel kitchens or campsite cooking areas to save on food costs.

4. Travel Off-Peak: Rates drop significantly during the late autumn and winter months.

Scotland's Diverse Accommodation Options

Scotland caters to all travelers, offering pet-friendly stays, budget hostels, and scenic campsites. Whether you're enjoying a Highland retreat with your pet or keeping costs low at a cozy hostel, proper planning ensures you'll have an amazing stay while experiencing the beauty and culture of Scotland.

DINING AND CUISINE IN SCOTLAND

Scotland's food scene is a delightful mix of traditional recipes, locally sourced ingredients, and modern culinary techniques. From hearty classics to Michelin-starred restaurants, the country offers something for every taste and budget. This guide introduces you to must-try Scottish dishes and some of the best dining options in Edinburgh and Glasgow.

Traditional Scottish Dishes You Must Try

1. Haggis

- **What It Is:** Scotland's national dish, made with sheep's heart, liver, and lungs, combined with oatmeal, spices, and onions. It's traditionally cooked in a sheep's stomach but modern versions often use a casing.

- **How It's Served**: Typically paired with "neeps and tatties" (mashed turnips and potatoes) and sometimes drizzled with whisky sauce.

- **Where to Try:** Many Scottish pubs and restaurants serve haggis, but local taverns often provide the most authentic experience.

2. Cullen Skink

- **What It Is:** A rich and creamy soup made with smoked haddock, potatoes, and onions.

- **Why You'll Love It:** It's comforting and filling, perfect for a cold day.

- **Where to Try**: Found in coastal towns or traditional seafood restaurants across Scotland.

3. Scotch Pie

- **What It Is:** A small savory pie filled with minced mutton or beef and encased in a flaky, hot water crust pastry.

- **How It's Enjoyed**: Popular as a snack or alongside a cup of tea.

- **Where to Try**: Available in bakeries and pie shops throughout Scotland.

4. Arbroath Smokies

- **What It Is:** Smoked haddock prepared using a traditional method unique to the town of Arbroath.

- **How It's Served:** Eaten on its own or incorporated into dishes like fishcakes and Cullen Skink.

- **Where to Try:** Best experienced in Arbroath or at seafood markets around the country.

5. Cranachan

- **What It Is:** A light dessert made with whipped cream, honey, raspberries, toasted oats, and a splash of whisky.

- **Why It's Special**: It's often served during Scottish celebrations.

- **Where to Try:** Available at traditional restaurants or during Burns Night dinners.

6. Sticky Toffee Pudding

- **What It Is:** A moist sponge cake made with dates and topped with a rich toffee sauce.

- **Why You'll Love It:** This sweet treat is perfect when paired with vanilla ice cream.

- **Where to Try:** Pubs and dessert menus across Scotland.

7. Whisky and Local Cheeses

- **What to Pair:** Scotland's famous whiskies complement local cheeses like Caboc, Lanark Blue, and Isle of Mull cheddar.

- **Where to Try:** Many whisky bars offer pairing menus to enhance the experience.

Top Restaurants in Edinburgh and Glasgow

Edinburgh's Dining Scene

Edinburgh's dining options blend the city's historical charm with modern culinary innovation, ranging from elegant fine dining to casual pubs.

1. The Kitchin

- **Type**: Michelin-star fine dining.

- **Cuisine**: Seasonal dishes featuring fresh Scottish ingredients.

- **Highlight**: The tasting menu with venison, seafood, and locally sourced produce.

- **Cost**: £80–£150 per person.

2. The Witchery by the Castle

- **Type**: Romantic fine dining.

- **Cuisine**: Traditional Scottish with an opulent ambiance.

- **Highlight**: The dramatic gothic décor paired with lamb shoulder or langoustines.

- **Cost**: £70–£120 per person.

3. Timberyard

- **Type**: Farm-to-table dining.

- **Cuisine**: Sustainable, seasonal, and creative.

- **Highlight**: A multi-course tasting menu focused on local ingredients.

- **Cost**: £60–£100 per person.

4. Scran & Scallie

- **Type**: Gastropub.

- **Cuisine**: Scottish comfort food with a modern twist.
- **Highlight**: Try the fish and chips or steak pie with a local craft ale.
- **Cost**: £25–£50 per person.

5. Oink

- **Type**: Quick-service dining.
- **Cuisine**: Specializing in roast hog rolls.
- **Highlight**: Perfect for a quick, hearty lunch while exploring the city.
- **Cost**: £5–£10 per person.

Glasgow's Dining Scene

Glasgow is known for its vibrant food culture, offering an exciting mix of Scottish classics and international flavors.

1. Cail Bruich

- **Type**: Michelin-star fine dining.

- **Cuisine**: Innovative modern Scottish.

- **Highlight**: The seasonal tasting menu featuring smoked scallops and venison.

- **Cost**: £100–£150 per person.

2. Ubiquitous Chip

- **Type**: Fine dining.

- **Cuisine**: Traditional Scottish with a creative edge.

- **Highlight**: Signature dishes like haggis and smoked salmon, served in a lush courtyard.

- **Cost**: £40–£80 per person.

3. The Finnieston

- **Type**: Seafood restaurant and bar.

- **Cuisine**: Scottish seafood paired with creative cocktails.

- **Highlight**: Try the oysters or lobster thermidor.

- **Cost**: £30–£70 per person.

4. Ox and Finch

- **Type**: Modern casual dining.

- **Cuisine**: Small plates inspired by global flavors.

- **Highlight**: Crowd favorites like duck breast and burrata.

- **Cost**: £25–£50 per person.

5. Mother India

- **Type**: Indian-Scottish fusion.

- **Cuisine**: Traditional Indian dishes with a twist, like spiced haggis pakoras.

- **Highlight**: Tapas-style dining perfect for sharing.

- **Cost**: £20–£40 per person.

Tips for Dining in Scotland

1. **Book Ahead:** Popular restaurants, especially Michelin-starred ones, require advance reservations.

2. **Visit Local Pubs:** For authentic Scottish dishes at affordable prices, explore local pubs.

3. **Ask the Locals:** Locals often know the best hidden gems for dining.

4. **Explore Street Food Markets**: Markets like Stockbridge in Edinburgh are great for sampling local flavors.

5. **Balance Your Budget:** Mix fine dining with casual options to enjoy a variety of experiences without overspending.

Scotland's diverse culinary scene has something to offer every traveler, whether you prefer comforting traditional dishes or elegant, innovative meals. From the hearty flavors of haggis to the indulgence of sticky toffee pudding, every bite in Scotland tells a story of tradition and creativity.

Seafood and Coastal Delicacies

Scotland's coastal regions are famous for their fresh seafood, making it a haven for seafood lovers. From bustling fish markets in Aberdeen to the charming harbors of the Outer Hebrides, Scotland's coastal cuisine highlights the bounty of its waters. The seafood here is prepared in ways that reflect the country's maritime traditions while embracing modern culinary creativity.

Why Choose Scotland's Seafood?

- **Freshness**: Most of Scotland's seafood is freshly caught daily, guaranteeing exceptional taste and quality.

- **Variety**: Scotland offers an impressive array of seafood, from succulent langoustines to flavorful oysters and premium salmon.

- **Heritage**: Recipes perfected over generations in fishing communities combine traditional methods with innovative flavors.

Must-Try Seafood Dishes in Scotland

1. Langoustines

Known as "Scampi," langoustines are a delicacy in Scotland.

- **How It's Served:** Grilled with garlic butter, in rich seafood platters, or added to soups.

- **Where to Try:** Find them in seafood restaurants in Oban or on the Isle of Mull.

2. Arbroath Smokies

A traditional delicacy of smoked haddock, prepared using a centuries-old method in Arbroath.

- **How It's Served:** Often enjoyed with bread and butter or as an ingredient in Cullen Skink soup.

- **Where to Try**: Visit Arbroath or local seafood markets to enjoy this dish at its best.

3. Scottish Salmon

Renowned for its rich flavor, Scottish salmon is a global favorite.

- **How It's Served:** Smoked, grilled, or cured, often paired with fresh vegetables.

- **Where to Try:** Enjoy it at fine dining restaurants, especially in Aberdeen or Edinburgh.

4. Oysters

Fresh Scottish oysters are a highlight of the coastal dining experience.

- **How It's Served**: Raw with lemon, grilled with herbs, or paired with whisky.

- **Where to Try:** Loch Fyne Oyster Bar is a prime spot for sampling these.

5. Lobster and Crab

Caught off Scotland's shores, these crustaceans are a staple of seafood menus.

- **How It's Served:** Grilled with butter, in hearty seafood platters, or as part of fresh salads.
- **Where to Try:** Visit coastal towns like Mallaig or Ullapool for the freshest catches.

Top Seafood Restaurants in Scotland

1. Loch Fyne Oyster Bar (Cairndow)

- Specialties: Oysters, smoked salmon, and fresh seafood platters.

- Cost: £30–£70 per person.

2. The Fish Market (Edinburgh)

- Specialties: Langoustines, freshly grilled fish, and classic fish and chips.
- Cost: £15–£40 per person.

3. Seafood Shack (Ullapool)

- Specialties: Casual dining with fresh, locally caught seafood.
- Cost: £10–£25 per person.

4. Creel Inn (Stonehaven)

- Specialties: Lobster, crab, and Arbroath Smokies.
- Cost: £25–£50 per person.

Tips for Enjoying Scottish Seafood

1. Visit Local Markets: Try fresh catches from markets in towns like Oban and Peterhead.

2. **Pair with Drinks:** Pair your meal with a local whisky or crisp white wine to enhance the flavors.

3. **Check Seasonal Availability:** Some seafood, like oysters, is best enjoyed during certain months.

Vegetarian and Vegan Dining Options

Scotland's vegetarian and vegan dining scene has grown significantly, offering creative dishes made with local produce. Whether you're in a city or a rural area, you'll find plenty of plant-based options to satisfy your appetite.

Why Scotland is Great for Plant-Based Dining

- **Local Ingredients:** Scotland's root vegetables, berries, and oats form the base of many vegetarian dishes.

- **Innovative Menus:** Chefs are transforming traditional recipes into vegetarian and vegan-friendly options.

- **Dedicated Restaurants**: Many cities, especially Edinburgh and Glasgow, feature exclusive vegetarian and vegan eateries.

Plant-Based Scottish Dishes

1. Vegetarian Haggis

- A meat-free version made with lentils, oats, and spices.
- **Where to Try:** Available in pubs and restaurants like Hendersons in Edinburgh.

2. Vegan Cranachan

A dessert made with coconut cream, raspberries, and toasted oats.

- **Where to Try:** Found on vegan menus in upscale restaurants.

3. Scottish Oatcakes with Vegan Cheese

- Oatcakes served with plant-based cheese spreads or chutneys.
- **Where to Try:** Available at farmers' markets or local cafés.

Top Vegetarian and Vegan Restaurants

(In Edinburgh):

1. Hendersons

- A pioneer in vegetarian dining with creative, plant-based dishes.
- Cost: £15–£30 per person.

2. Holy Cow

- A casual café offering vegan burgers and desserts.
- Cost: £10–£20 per person.

(In Glasgow):

1. Mono

- A trendy café with hearty vegan dishes like pizzas and stews.
- Cost: £15–£30 per person.

2. The 78

- A vibrant vegan bar serving comfort food like mac and cheese.

- Cost: £10–£25 per person.

(In Inverness):

1. The Olive Tree Café

- Known for its vegetarian breakfast and fresh lunch options.

- Cost: £10–£20 per person.

Tips for Plant-Based Travelers

1. Look for Menus Online: Many restaurants now label vegetarian and vegan dishes clearly.

2. Visit Farmers' Markets: Explore fresh produce and artisanal vegan treats.

3. Request Customizations: Many chefs are happy to adapt dishes to suit dietary needs.

Scotland's culinary offerings range from fresh seafood to creative plant-based dishes, catering to all tastes. Whether you're enjoying lobster by the coast or trying vegan haggis in Edinburgh, Scotland's food scene is sure to impress.

PRACTICAL INFORMATION AND TRAVEL TIPS

Traveling in Scotland is an incredible experience with its breathtaking landscapes, rich history, and welcoming people. To ensure your trip goes smoothly, it's important to understand basic details like currency, driving rules, and ways to travel sustainably. Here's a straightforward guide to help you enjoy Scotland with ease.

Currency, Tipping, and Language

Currency:

- Scotland uses British Pounds (£), with common notes like £5, £10, £20, and £50.

- Scottish banks issue their own notes, which are accepted across the UK but may occasionally raise questions outside of Scotland.

Helpful Tips:

- Credit and debit cards are widely accepted, even in rural areas.

- ATMs are easy to find, but check if your card provider charges fees for international transactions.

Tipping:

- Tipping is appreciated but not compulsory.

- Restaurants: Leave a 10–15% tip if service isn't already added to the bill.

- Taxis: Round up the fare or add 10%.

- Hotels: Tip porters or housekeepers around £1–£2 for their services.

Language:

- English is the main language spoken everywhere in Scotland.

- You may also see Scottish Gaelic on road signs, especially in the Highlands and islands, and some locals speak it fluently.

Emergency Contacts and Healthcare

Emergency Numbers:

- Dial 999 or 112 for police, fire, ambulance, or coast guard emergencies.

- For non-emergencies, contact 101 for the police or 111 for health advice through NHS 24.

Healthcare:

- Scotland provides free healthcare through the NHS for UK residents and visitors.

- EU visitors can use an EHIC or GHIC card for medical services.

Tips for Visitors:

•Travel insurance is highly recommended to cover private healthcare or unexpected costs.

•Always carry essential medications, clearly labeled, along with any necessary prescriptions.

Pharmacies:

Pharmacies (called "Chemists") are located in towns and cities, offering over-the-counter medication and professional advice.

Driving Tips for Scotland's Roads

Driving in Scotland gives you the freedom to explore its natural beauty, but it's important to know the rules and road conditions.

Driving Rules:

- Drive on the left-hand side of the road.
- Seat belts are mandatory for all passengers.

Speed limits:

- 30 mph (48 km/h) in towns and cities.
- 60 mph (96 km/h) on single-lane roads.
- 70 mph (112 km/h) on motorways and dual carriageways.

Using a mobile phone while driving is illegal unless it's hands-free.

Road Conditions:

- Rural roads can be narrow and winding, especially in the Highlands and islands.

- Be aware of single-track roads with passing places. Let uphill or larger vehicles pass first.

Parking:

- Paid parking is common in cities; always check signs for restrictions.

- Parking in rural areas is often free, though spaces may be limited.

Fuel:

Fill your tank before heading to remote areas, as fuel stations can be sparse.

Helpful Tips:

- Check weather forecasts before driving, especially in winter, as snow and rain can make roads slippery.

- Renting a smaller car is better for navigating narrow roads, and ensure your rental includes insurance.

Sustainable Travel Practices in Scotland

Scotland's natural beauty is a key attraction, and sustainable travel helps preserve it for future generations.

Sustainability Tips:

1. Reduce Carbon Footprint:

- Use public transport like buses and trains, which are efficient and eco-friendly.

- Opt for carpooling or hire an electric vehicle for longer trips.

2. Respect Nature:

- Stay on marked trails when hiking to protect fragile ecosystems.

- Avoid littering; always dispose of waste properly or take it with you.

3. **Support Local Communities:**

- Stay in locally owned accommodations such as guesthouses or B&Bs.

- Buy from farmers' markets or small shops to support local businesses.

4. **Limit Plastic Use:**

- Bring a reusable water bottle and refill it at public fountains.

- Use reusable shopping bags for groceries and souvenirs.

5. **Protect Wildlife:**

- Observe animals from a distance without disturbing their habitats.

- Never feed wild animals as it disrupts their natural behaviors.

Additional Practical Tips

1. **Wi-Fi and Connectivity:**

- Most hotels, restaurants, and public spaces offer free Wi-Fi.

- Consider getting a local SIM card for affordable data plans.

2. Weather Preparedness:

- Scotland's weather is unpredictable, so pack a waterproof jacket and layers no matter the season.

3. Accessibility:

- Many attractions are wheelchair-friendly, but it's best to check ahead or contact venues for specific details.

4. Public Transport:

- Scotland's train and bus networks connect major cities and rural areas.

- Get a Spirit of Scotland Travelpass for unlimited travel over several days.

Traveling in Scotland is a rewarding experience with its stunning landscapes, warm culture, and fascinating history. Following these tips will help you make the most of your trip while staying safe, comfortable, and mindful of the environment. Whether you're navigating winding roads, enjoying local delicacies, or hiking in the Highlands, Scotland promises unforgettable memories for every traveler.

INDEX

A comprehensive alphabetical listing of the key locations, attractions, and topics covered in this guide ensures easy reference for travelers. This section helps you quickly find the information you need about Scotland's destinations, dining, accommodations, and travel tips.

A

Abbotsford House: Exploring the Borders

Accommodation Options: Pet-Friendly Stays, Castles, Luxury Hotels, Budget-Friendly Hostels

Arbroath Smokies: Seafood Delicacies

Argyll: Barcaldine Castle, Isle of Eriska Hotel

Applecross Peninsula: Scenic Highland Retreat

Attractions: Top Sites in Edinburgh, Glasgow, Highlands

B

Balmoral Hotel: Luxury Stays in Edinburgh

Beaches: West Sands Beach, Luskentyre Beach

Ben Nevis: Outdoor Adventures, Glen Nevis Campsite

Borders Region: Abbotsford House, Melrose Abbey

Borthwick Castle: Historic Accommodation

C

Castles: Inverlochy, Dalhousie, Barcaldine

Coastal Delicacies: Langoustines, Oysters, Lobster

Cullen Skink: Traditional Scottish Dish

Culross: Historic Village Exploration

Currency: British Pound, Tipping Guidelines

D

Driving Tips: Scotland's Roads and Single-Track Routes

Dunvegan Castle: Isle of Skye Highlights

Dining: Traditional Dishes, Vegetarian Options, Top Restaurants

E

Emergency Contacts: Police, Ambulance, Healthcare Assistance

Edinburgh: Royal Mile, Holyrood Palace, The Kitchin Restaurant

Eilean Donan Castle: Scenic Highlands Fortress

F

Fairy Pools: Isle of Skye's Natural Wonders

Fife Arms: Boutique Hotel in Braemar

Fish Markets: Fresh Seafood in Aberdeen, Ullapool

Fort Augustus: Loch Ness Adventures

G

Glen Coe: Scenic Treasure in the Highlands

Gleneagles Hotel: Luxurious Countryside Accommodation

Great Glen: Loch Ness, Outdoor Activities

Gaelic Language: Linguistic Heritage of Scotland

Glasgow: Kelvingrove Museum, Riverside Museum

H

Haggis: Iconic Scottish Dish

Highland Games: Cultural Festivals and Events

Highlands: Scenic Drives, Castles, Nature Walks

Hiking Trails: West Highland Way, Quiraing, Old Man of Storr

Holy Cow: Vegan Dining in Edinburgh

I

Inverness: Castle, River Ness Walk, Gateway to Loch Ness

Isle of Skye: Fairy Pools, Dunvegan Castle, Portree

Islands: Shetland, Orkney, Hebrides

K

Kelpies: Iconic Horse Head Sculptures

Killiehuntly Farmhouse: Boutique Accommodation in Cairngorms

L

Langoustines: Seafood Specialty

Loch Lomond: National Park Camping, Scenic Walks

Loch Ness: Nessie Legends, Urquhart Castle

Loch Fyne: Oysters, Seafood Dining

M

Melrose Abbey: Borders Region Landmark

Mono: Vegan Dining in Glasgow

Museums: Edinburgh Castle Exhibits, Glasgow's Riverside Museum

N

National Parks: Loch Lomond, Cairngorms

Nature Watching: Puffins, Dolphins, Red Deer

O

Oysters: Coastal Dining Highlight

Oban: Seafood Hub, Youth Hostels

P

Pet-Friendly Stays: Hotels, Cabins, and Cottages

Plockton: Quaint Highland Village

Portree: Isle of Skye's Main Town

R

River Ness: Scenic Walks in Inverness

Royal Mile: Edinburgh's Historic Heart

S

Seafood Shack: Casual Dining in Ullapool

Scottish Borders: Abbotsford House, Historic Sites

Sustainable Travel: Eco-Friendly Practices and Tips

T

Tipping: Customs for Restaurants, Taxis, and Hotels

Trossachs: Scenic Trails and Lochside Views

Traditional Dishes: Haggis, Cranachan, Scotch Pie

U

Urquhart Castle: Loch Ness Exploration

V

Vegetarian Dining: Vegan Restaurants, Plant-Based Haggis

Viaduct: Jacobite Steam Train Crossing

W

West Sands Beach: St. Andrews Coastal Attraction

Whisky Tasting: Distilleries in Speyside, Islay, and Highlands

Wildlife: Watching Puffins, Eagles, and Seals

Y

Youth Hostels: Budget Accommodations in Oban, Edinburgh

This index ensures you can quickly navigate through Scotland's many highlights, making planning and exploring even easier.

LOCATIONS & COORDINATES

I'll compile the detailed locations, addresses, and coordinates for all Top Attractions, Hidden Gems, and Accommodations mentioned in the above contents. This information will ensure easy access for planning your visit.

Top Attractions

Edinburgh Castle

- Location: Castlehill, Edinburgh EH1 2NG, Scotland

- Coordinates: 55.9486° N, 3.1999° W

The Royal Mile and Holyrood Palace

- Location: Canongate, Edinburgh EH8 8DX, Scotland

- Coordinates: 55.9517° N, 3.1726° W

Loch Ness and Urquhart Castle

- Urquhart Castle Location: Drumnadrochit, Inverness IV63 6XJ, Scotland

- Coordinates: 57.3244° N, 4.4402° W

Stirling Castle and Wallace Monument

- Stirling Castle Location: Castle Esplanade, Stirling FK8 1EJ, Scotland

- Coordinates: 56.1236° N, 3.9470° W

- Wallace Monument Location: Abbey Craig, Hillfoots Rd, Stirling FK9 5LF, Scotland

- Coordinates: 56.1481° N, 3.9360° W

The Isle of Skye's Breathtaking Landscapes

- Fairy Pools Location: Glen Brittle, Isle of Skye IV47 8TA, Scotland

- Coordinates: 57.2503° N, 6.2722° W

Hidden Gems

Glen Coe

- Location: Ballachulish PH49 4HX, Scotland

- Coordinates: 56.6824° N, 5.1023° W

Eilean Donan Castle

- Location: Dornie, Kyle of Lochalsh IV40 8DX, Scotland
- Coordinates: 57.2741° N, 5.5163° W

The Kelpies and Falkirk Wheel

- The Kelpies Location: The Helix, Falkirk FK2 7ZT, Scotland
- Coordinates: 56.0157° N, 3.7542° W
- Falkirk Wheel Location: Lime Rd, Tamfourhill, Falkirk FK1 4RS, Scotland
- Coordinates: 56.0026° N, 3.8415° W

Plockton

- Location: Plockton, Wester Ross, IV52 8TN, Scotland
- Coordinates: 57.3382° N, 5.6546° W

Culross

- Location: Culross, Fife KY12 8JH, Scotland

- Coordinates: 56.0555° N, 3.6297° W

Accommodations

Luxury Hotels

1. The Balmoral Hotel

- Address: 1 Princes St, Edinburgh EH2 2EQ, Scotland

- Coordinates: 55.9527° N, 3.1890° W

2. Gleneagles Hotel

- Address: Auchterarder, Perthshire PH3 1NF, Scotland

- Coordinates: 56.2953° N, 3.7470° W

3. Isle of Eriska Hotel

- Address: Benderloch, Oban PA37 1SD, Scotland

- Coordinates: 56.5389° N, 5.4036° W

Boutique Hotels

1. The Witchery by the Castle

- Address: Castlehill, Edinburgh EH1 2NF, Scotland
- Coordinates: 55.9486° N, 3.2003° W

2. The Fife Arms

- Address: Mar Rd, Braemar AB35 5YN, Scotland
- Coordinates: 57.0051° N, 3.4017° W

3. Killiehuntly Farmhouse

- Address: Kingussie PH21 1NX, Scotland
- Coordinates: 57.0724° N, 4.0449° W

Castle Stays

1. Inverlochy Castle Hotel

- Address: Torlundy, Fort William PH33 6SN, Scotland

- Coordinates: 56.8437° N, 5.0616° W

2. Dalhousie Castle

- Address: Cockpen Rd, Bonnyrigg EH19 3JB, Scotland

- Coordinates: 55.8627° N, 3.0875° W

3. Barcaldine Castle

- Address: Benderloch, Oban PA37 1SA, Scotland

- Coordinates: 56.5050° N, 5.3977° W

4. Borthwick Castle

- Address: North Middleton, Gorebridge EH23 4QY, Scotland

- Coordinates: 55.8352° N, 2.9887° W

Pet-Friendly Stays

1. The Four Seasons Hotel

- Address: Lochside, St Fillans, Loch Earn, Crieff PH6 2NF, Scotland

- Coordinates: 56.3906° N, 4.2067° W

2. The Inn on the Tay

- Address: Grandtully, Pitlochry PH9 0PL, Scotland

- Coordinates: 56.6354° N, 3.7998° W

Budget Hostels

1. Castle Rock Hostel

- Address: 15 Johnston Terrace, Edinburgh EH1 2PW, Scotland

- Coordinates: 55.9488° N, 3.1953° W

2. Oban Youth Hostel

- Address: Corran Esplanade, Oban PA34 5AF, Scotland

- Coordinates: 56.4122° N, 5.4723° W

3. Skye Basecamp Hostel

- Address: Broadford, Isle of Skye IV49 9AE, Scotland

- Coordinates: 57.2381° N, 5.9155° W

These detailed addresses and coordinates will help you efficiently plan your visit to Scotland.

MAP/QR CODE

Don't forget to Scan

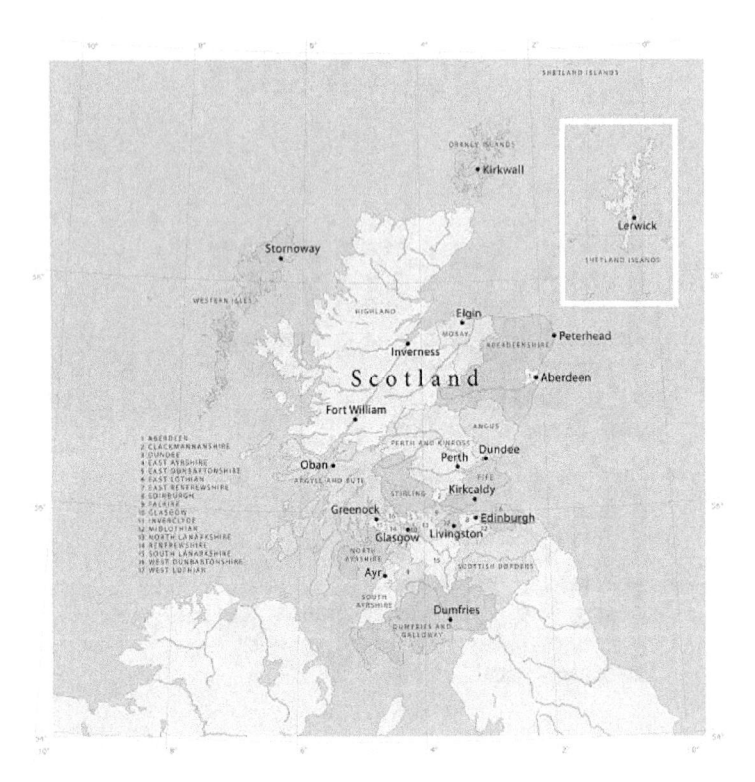

NORTH ATLANTIC OCEAN
ORKNEY ISLANDS
Mainland
Kirkwall
SHETLAND ISLANDS
Mainland
Lerwick
Thurso
Lewis with Harris
Stornoway
North Uist
South Uist
Skye
HEBRIDES
Mull
Islay
Arran
SCOTLAND
Inverness
Loch Ness
Aberdeen
Fort William
Dundee
Perth
Saint Andrews
Kirkcaldy
EDINBURGH
Glasgow
Ayr
Stranraer
NORTH SEA
Northern Ireland
Belfast
England
UNITED KINGDOM
Isle of Man
Douglas
IRELAND